Diplomacy: A Very Short Introduction

'A veteran international historian, Siracusa presents a masterly account of diplomacy through analyzing well selected issues from the era of the American Revolution to the age of globalization.'
Sadao Asada, Professor Emeritus of International History, Doshisha University, Kyoto, Japan

D0054982

VERY SHORT INTRODUCTIONS are for anyone wanting a stimulating and accessible way in to a new subject. They are written by experts, and have been published in more than 25 languages worldwide.

The series began in 1995, and now represents a wide variety of topics in history, philosophy, religion, science, and the humanities. The VSI Library now contains over 200 volumes—a Very Short Introduction to everything from ancient Egypt and Indian philosophy to conceptual art and cosmology—and will continue to grow to a library of around 300 titles.

Very Short Introductions available now:

ADVERTISING Winston Fletcher
AFRICAN HISTORY John Parker and
    Richard Rathbone
AMERICAN POLITICAL PARTIES
    AND ELECTIONS L. Sandy Maisel
THE AMERICAN PRESIDENCY
    Charles O. Jones
ANARCHISM Colin Ward
ANCIENT EGYPT Ian Shaw
ANCIENT PHILOSOPHY
    Julia Annas
ANCIENT WARFARE
    Harry Sidebottom
ANGLICANISM Mark Chapman
THE ANGLO-SAXON AGE
    John Blair
ANIMAL RIGHTS David DeGrazia
ANTISEMITISM Steven Beller
THE APOCRYPHAL GOSPELS
    Paul Foster
ARCHAEOLOGY Paul Bahn
ARCHITECTURE Andrew Ballantyne
ARISTOTLE Jonathan Barnes
ART HISTORY Dana Arnold
ART THEORY Cynthia Freeland
ATHEISM Julian Baggini
AUGUSTINE Henry Chadwick
AUTISM Uta Frith
BARTHES Jonathan Culler
BESTSELLERS John Sutherland
THE BIBLE John Riches
BIBLICAL ARCHAEOLOGY
    Eric H. Cline

BIOGRAPHY Hermione Lee
THE BOOK OF MORMON
    Terryl Givens
THE BRAIN Michael O'Shea
BRITISH POLITICS Anthony Wright
BUDDHA Michael Carrithers
BUDDHISM Damien Keown
BUDDHIST ETHICS Damien Keown
CAPITALISM James Fulcher
CATHOLICISM Gerald O'Collins
THE CELTS Barry Cunliffe
CHAOS Leonard Smith
CHOICE THEORY Michael Allingham
CHRISTIAN ART Beth Williamson
CHRISTIANITY Linda Woodhead
CITIZENSHIP Richard Bellamy
CLASSICAL MYTHOLOGY
    Helen Morales
CLASSICS Mary Beard and
    John Henderson
CLAUSEWITZ Michael Howard
THE COLD WAR Robert McMahon
COMMUNISM Leslie Holmes
CONSCIOUSNESS Susan Blackmore
CONTEMPORARY ART
    Julian Stallabrass
CONTINENTAL PHILOSOPHY
    Simon Critchley
COSMOLOGY Peter Coles
THE CRUSADES
    Christopher Tyerman
CRYPTOGRAPHY Fred Piper
    and Sean Murphy

For more information visit our web site
www.oup.co.uk/general/vsi/

Joseph M. Siracusa

DIPLOMACY

A Very Short Introduction

OXFORD
UNIVERSITY PRESS

Great Clarendon Street, Oxford OX2 6DP

Oxford University Press is a department of the University of Oxford.
It furthers the University's objective of excellence in research, scholarship,
and education by publishing worldwide in

Oxford New York

Auckland Cape Town Dar es Salaam Hong Kong Karachi
Kuala Lumpur Madrid Melbourne Mexico City Nairobi
New Delhi Shanghai Taipei Toronto

With offices in

Argentina Austria Brazil Chile Czech Republic France Greece
Guatemala Hungary Italy Japan Poland Portugal Singapore
South Korea Switzerland Thailand Turkey Ukraine Vietnam

Oxford is a registered trade mark of Oxford University Press
in the UK and in certain other countries

Published in the United States
by Oxford University Press Inc., New York

British Library Cataloguing in Publication Data

Data available

Library of Congress Cataloging in Publication Data

Data available

Typeset by SPI Publisher Services, Pondicherry, India
Printed in Great Britain by
Ashford Colour Press Ltd, Gosport, Hampshire

ISBN 978-0-19-958850-3

1 3 5 7 9 10 8 6 4 2

To the memory of my father

Contents

Preface

Diplomacy – not unlike some other ancient professions – has been around a very long time. David Reynolds dates its origins back to at least the Bronze Age; documents from the Euphrates kingdom in the mid-8th century BC and from Akhenaten's Egypt four centuries later reveal a world of peripatetic envoys, prompted by matters of peace and war. It was primitive by today's standards, there were few rules, distances were formidable, but it was a recognizable form of diplomacy. Since then, diplomacy has evolved greatly, coming to mean different things, to different people, at different times, ranging from the elegant ('the management of relations between independent states by the process of negotiations': Harold Nicolson) to the inelegant ('the art of saying nice "doggie" until you can find a rock': Wynn Catlin). Whatever one's definition, few could doubt that the course and consequences of the major events of modern international diplomacy have shaped and changed the global world in which we live.

It is the purpose of this book to introduce the general reader to the subject and study of diplomacy, from an historical perspective. Based on examples taken from significant historical phases and episodes, it is designed to illustrate the art of diplomacy in action, which should at once engage and instruct, while simultaneously bringing out changes in method at key historical junctures. I am not setting out to give the reader a history of diplomacy, but rather a sense of the ways in which the practice of diplomacy varies at particular historical moments. Diplomacy has its own history, of course, as institutions change and new resources become available over time. But here, I want to use particular case studies to bring out the very different demands that circumstances make on the practice of diplomats. I also want to give some sense of the way in which skilful diplomacy, as well as rashness, excessive caution, and clumsiness, can have important ramifications for the fate of nations. Put another way, the case studies chosen here will demonstrate that diplomacy was and is an important element of statecraft, and that without skilful diplomacy political success may remain elusive.

Within this context, we will look briefly at the evolution of modern diplomacy, focusing on diplomats and what they do, paying particular attention to the art of treaty-making; the diplomacy of the American Revolution, which heralded the fateful disruption of the British Empire in the 1770s; the diplomatic origins of the Great War and its aftermath Versailles, which carried away four empires and an entire generation of young men; the personal summitry behind the night Stalin and Churchill divided Europe, which foreshadowed the coming of the Cold War; the asymmetrical diplomacy behind the making of ANZUS – or the Australian–New Zealand–United States Security Treaty, which has endured for over fifty years; and, finally, the diplomacy of the global economic system, comprising, *inter alia*, the activities of transnational corporations and intergovernmental organizations, as well as the diplomacy of civil society organizations, which opened up new pathways for the conduct of diplomacy while facilitating the involvement of new participants.

After factoring out the obvious differences such as the various systems of government that each age of diplomacy represented and the communications revolution that was profoundly important, especially for modern summitry, what each of these case studies has in common is the universal role of negotiations. In the chapters that follow, the diplomat *qua* negotiator always set out to achieve an agreement or understanding which was somewhat better than the realities of his fundamental position would have justified and which, in any case, would have been no worse than his fundamental position would have required. This is as true in relations between nation-states as in relations between organizations and individuals. Not all succeeded, of course – some more than others. Meanwhile, each had to make sure of his constituency while making equally sure that his opposite number had control of his. Among the cases under consideration, high marks go to the diplomats of the American Revolution whose realism compelled them to think and act in terms of power, rightfully eschewing ideology and moral principles. There was, in fact, precious little room to manoeuvre, and the fear of failure was a constant companion. Benjamin Franklin's timely warning that the colonies either could hang together or one at a time ultimately translated itself into the brilliant outcome achieved by the revolutionary diplomats who seldom failed to take advantage of Europe's distresses. And this was all done at a time when it could take a month or more for a letter to travel from Philadelphia to Paris!

And, like the other diplomatic episodes found in this volume, the historical repercussions could be profound. The disruption of the British Empire in the 1770s, for example, was one of the fateful events of modern history. Had British statesmanship then been capable of the levels of wisdom it attained in the next century, a British–American or American–British Commonwealth of Nations might have guided the world along paths of peaceful development with little to fear from Imperial Germany, Nazi Germany, or a Communist Russia. Such a might-have-been is the stuff of virtual history and an endless, fascinating subject of speculation. Similarly, the best statecraft of Bismarck's classic diplomacy in the run-up to the 20th century could do nothing to avoid the drift towards the abyss of war. Consequently, as historian Arnold Toynbee so aptly writes, Western civilization was about to enter a 'time of troubles', comparable to the self-destructive rage that afflicted the city-states of ancient Greece. Or, to quote Henry Kissinger: 'Since nothing about the First World War had gone as planned, it was inevitable that the quest for peace would prove as futile as the expectations with which nations had launched themselves into the catastrophe.' For all their efforts, the diplomats at Versailles achieved the precise opposite of what they had set out to do, inexorably, tragically laying the groundwork for the next, more horrible world war. In this sense, then, the story of diplomacy also reads as a cautionary tale.

Apropos acknowledgements, I should first of all like to express my gratitude to my friend and colleague Manfred Steger for suggesting this topic and Andrea Keegan, Luciana O'Flaherty, and Emma Marchant at Oxford University Press for making it happen. I should also like to thank Sandra Assersohn for providing the images and accompanying captions that grace the following chapters. I should also be remiss if I did not thank the anonymous Delegates for their thoughtful reports and constructive suggestions. Even those who did not much agree with me gave me much food for thought. My intellectual debts are at once overwhelming and obvious, and are recognized in the text and References and further reading. Needless to say – but I will say it anyway – I am alone responsible for the text that follows.

Professor Joseph M. Siracusa
Melbourne

List of illustrations

Chapter 1
Evolution of diplomacy

Traditional diplomacy has been most importantly concerned with the transition from a state of peace to a state of war, and vice versa; in other words, dealing with the interface of conflict and peace-making. And while this is a central aspect of diplomatic activities in the past and present, it should also be noted that it is today only one, important, aspect. Diplomacy has become something very much more than the diplomacy of states and governments. Though it is still true that the legal formalities based on the 1961 Vienna Convention on Diplomatic Relations acknowledge only the diplomacy of states, on the ground, it is impossible to ignore the diplomacy of the global economic system, from the activities of TNCs (transnational corporations) to the intervention of the global economic IGOs (intergovernmental organizations), particularly the World Trade Organization. These, in turn, have diplomatic webs which operate both within and outside the traditional diplomatic system. The same is true of another vast area of diplomatic activity, the diplomacy of civil society organizations. Moreover, the saga of failed and failing states, civil conflict, and international terrorism has in reality created a radically new global world of urgent communications between states and NGOs (non-governmental organizations), between NGOs and IGOs, and amongst NGOs themselves. These developments will be dealt with later (see Chapter 6).

The evolution of diplomacy

The roots of the word 'diplomacy' can be traced back to the ancient Greeks – the normal word for a diplomat in Classical Greece was, in fact, the word for an old man – and was later used by the French (*diplomatie*) to refer to the work of a negotiator. There is, of course, a long history of diplomatic activity going back literally thousands of years. The earliest diplomatic record extant is a letter inscribed on a tablet which has been dated some time around 2,500 BC, found in present-day northern Iran; it apparently was carried by an emissary who had made a round trip of nearly 1,200 miles between distant kingdoms. Sovereigns traditionally sent envoys to other sovereigns for various reasons: to prevent wars, cease hostilities, conclude treaties, or merely continue peaceful relations and further trade. The modern era of diplomacy is conventionally dated to the Peace of Westphalia in 1648, which ended hostilities in the Thirty Years War. It also established the independence of states and the notion of religious freedom and toleration. The first foreign ministry was created in 1626 by France's Cardinal Richelieu, who also introduced the classic approach to international relations, based on the nation-state and motivated by national interest as its ultimate goal. In the 18th century, Great Britain placed its diplomacy in the service of the balance of power, while in the 19th century, Metternich's Austria used its diplomacy to reconstruct the Concert of Europe, only to have it dismantled by Bismarck's Germany, reshaping European diplomacy, in Henry Kissinger's words, 'into a cold-blooded game of power politics'.

As divine-right kings gave way to constitutional monarchies and republics, embassies and legations became more and more institutionalized all over Europe, and by the end of the 19th century, European-style diplomacy had been adopted throughout the world. It was a fully fledged diplomatic system. Large countries had embassies in other large countries and legations in smaller

1. Cardinal Richelieu

countries. Embassies were headed by ambassadors and legations by ministers. Whether a particular diplomatic mission was given the rank of an embassy or legation – whether its chief was an ambassador or minister – formerly depended upon the importance that the two governments attached to their mutual relations. During the first century of its existence, for example, the United States maintained only legations abroad, and, reciprocally, foreign governments kept only legations in the American capital. In 1893, Congress provided for the elevation of several of the more important legations to embassies, on a reciprocal basis. Thereafter, embassies gradually replaced legations until 1966, when the last American legations (Bulgaria and Hungary) became embassies. The change was indicative of the growing importance that the United States attached to its diplomacy.

Public diplomacy

Embassies and legations were strictly limited in their contacts with the ordinary citizens of the host state. These limitations were eventually codified in the Havana Convention of 1928, which under the heading 'Duties of Diplomatic Officers' required that these officers were not to interfere in the internal affairs of the host state and must confine their relations to official communications. Thus, diplomatic personnel from abroad had no formal relations with the public at large in the receiving state. Prior to World War II, then, diplomacy was essentially a government-to-government relationship, in the sense that Foreign Diplomatic Officers were discouraged from participating in the domestic or foreign policies of the state in which they exercised their function. However, the Convention manifestly did not go so far as to say diplomats should have no contact with foreign citizens. This would have been unrealistic, since reporting on conditions in states of their accreditation has been a recognized function of resident missions since their invention in the 15th century, and they could have hardly done this without meeting with private citizens, albeit usually those confined to the local political, commercial, and financial elites. The stipulation restricting 'official communications' to foreign ministries was designed chiefly to protect the position of such ministries relative to other ministries – not relative to the citizenry in general – and thereby avoid chaos in bilateral relations.

Since the end of World War II, and for a number of reasons, especially the pressures of the Cold War and now the international war on terror, the practice of diplomacy has been broadened to include a distinctive government-to-people connection, broadly known as public diplomacy. It basically refers to the influence of public attitudes on the formation and execution of foreign policies. Coined in 1965 by Edmund Gullion, a US career diplomat, public diplomacy literally reaches beyond traditional diplomacy, aiming at the cultivation by governments of public opinion in other countries. Equally important, it openly sponsors the interaction of private groups and interests in one country with those of another, facilitated by the transnational flow of information and ideas.

Public diplomacy, according to Charles Wolf and Brian Rosen, can best be understood by contrasting its principal characteristics with those of *official* diplomacy. First, public diplomacy is transparent and widely disseminated, whereas official diplomacy is not; second, public diplomacy is transmitted by governments to wider, or in some cases selected, publics (especially those in the Middle East or the Muslim world), whereas official diplomacy is transmitted by governments to other governments; and, third, the themes and issues with which official diplomacy is concerned relate to the behaviour and policies of governments, whereas the themes and issues with which public diplomacy is concerned relate to the attitudes and behaviours of publics. Always open to charges of propaganda and interference in the internal affairs of other nations, public diplomacy challenged both the spirit and letter of the Havana Convention.

Diplomats and treaties

Traditional diplomacy has also been greatly concerned with making treaties. The *Oxford English Dictionary* defines 'treaty' variously: in a narrow sense, as a 'contract between two or more states, relating to peace, truce alliance, commerce or other international relations', and, more broadly, as 'a settlement or arrangement arrived at by treaty or negotiating, in the sense of an agreement, covenant, or contract'. It could have also said something about the distinction between the specific meanings of 'convention' and 'treaty', but it didn't. Whereas in the 19th century, the term 'convention' was regularly employed for bilateral agreements, in the 20th century it was generally employed for formal multilateral treaties, with a broad number of parties. Usually the instruments negotiated under the auspices of an international organization such as the United Nations are often entitled 'conventions'. In bilateral relations, the term is often applied to treaties of a technical or social character such as those on social security or double taxation.

Whichever name is used, the power to enter into treaty relations – the most formal and highest instrument of agreement between nations, almost always undertaken by diplomatic practitioners – is an essential attribute of sovereignty. The principle that treaties validly concluded are binding on the signatories, who must adhere to them in good faith, is a cardinal rule in international law. It is also the very basis of the modern system of international relations. The usual conditions essential to the valid conclusion of a treaty are that the contracting parties have the requisite capacity to enter into international engagements, the pleniopotentiaries who negotiate them must be properly authorized, and there is freedom of action on the part of the signatory powers. It is also recognized that a treaty is void if its conclusions have been procured by the threat or use of force in violation of the principles of international law embodied in the United Nations Charter. Peace treaties concluded after cessation of hostilities were usually considered to be valid because of preceding warfare. Nevertheless, the United States established a policy not to recognize any treaty or agreement brought about by means contrary to the Kellogg–Briand Pact (1928) – or Peace of Paris – by which the USA joined the other nations of the world in renouncing war as an instrument of national policy. The principle is known as the Stimson Doctrine, named after the Secretary of State Henry Stimson, who in 1931 formally expressed American opposition to the Japanese conquest of Manchuria, while refusing to accept any changes in territorial possession as a consequence of the invasion. The Stimson Doctrine was adopted by the League of Nations. Similar principles were included in the 1969 Vienna Convention on the Law of Treaties.

On the international level, the scope of the treaty-making power of a state is practically unlimited. It includes the acquisition of foreign territory, the cession of domestic territory, the delimitation and rectification of boundaries, the promise of mutual assistance, the guarantee of foreign investments, and the extradition of persons accused or convicted of crimes. Treaties may be of a law-making character and of a multinational nature, such as the conventions on the law of the sea and on the privileges and immunities of diplomatic missions and their staff. Multilateral treaties are also the basis for the establishment of international organizations and the determination of their individual functions and powers.

Many treaties can be classified as either political or commercial arrangements. Political treaties especially may relate to mutual defence in case of an armed attack; to guarantees of a particular state, such as neutrality; or to the preservation of existing boundaries. In particular, this concept of collective security – the idea of a universal, permanent, and collective commitment to oppose aggression while guaranteeing security – was an important innovation of 20th-century international relations. It was embedded in the Covenant of the League of Nations (Article X), at the insistence of Woodrow Wilson, and re-emerged in a modified form in the United Nations Charter. Commercial treaties usually provide mutual economic advantage, such as reduced tariffs on the imported products of the parties to the agreement. In modern times, such treaties often contain a clause stipulating that each signatory will extend to every other signatory treatment equally favourable to that accorded to any other national (the 'most-favoured-nation' clause). The most important multilateral treaty of that type is the General Agreement on Tariff and Trades (GATT). Another class of treaties provides for the submission of disputes to arbitration by special tribunals or to adjudication by institutions such as the Permanent Court of Arbitration or International Court of Justice.

International law prescribes neither a fixed form for a treaty nor any fixed procedure for its conclusion. It may be concluded by an exchange of diplomatic notes incorporating an agreed-upon text signed by authorized officials, or by the signing of one or more copies of the text by officials authorized to express the consent of their respective governments to be bound by the treaty. Many important treaties require ratification by each of the contracting parties. In such cases, the negotiators, after reaching agreement on the final text, sign the document and then submit the proposed treaty for ratification to the constitutionally authorized authority, usually the head of state or head of the government. In some countries – and some times – the procedures are easy and predictable. When the supreme leader of the Soviet Union, Joseph Stalin, wanted a non-aggression pact with Adolph Hitler in 1939 (the Nazi–Soviet Pact), there were no bars or procedures. In other places, the treaty process becomes quite complex and politically charged, and the outcome uncertain.

Treaties are considered binding (*pacta sunt servanda*) but may be terminated in various ways. The treaty itself may provide for its termination at a specified time, or it may allow one party to give notice of termination, effective either at the time of receipt or following the expiration of a specified period. A treaty may be terminated by one signatory's repudiation of its obligation; such a unilateral termination, however, may provoke retaliatory measures. A treaty may lapse naturally, through war or renunciation, or at other times by reliance on the principle *rebus sic stantibus* (things remaining that way), that is, when the state of affairs assumed by the signatory parties (when they signed the treaty, and therefore the real basis of the treaty) no longer exists and a substantial change in conditions has taken place. Notably, the doctrine of changed circumstances leading to termination is not generally applied to fundamental treaties of communal application such as the United Nations Charter or the Geneva Conventions. Examples of both abound in diplomatic history: Imperial Japan and Nazi Germany both gave formal notice to quit the League of Nations, while the great Cold War alliance arrangements such as SEATO and the Warsaw Pact fell away. More recently, the United States served notice that it was quitting the ABM (Anti-Ballistic Missile) Treaty with the former Soviet Union, the Russian Federation.

The Vienna Convention on the Law of Treaties

Rules of international law governing the conclusion, validity, effects, interpretation, modification, suspension, and termination of treaties were codified in the Vienna Convention on the Law of Treaties, adopted in 1969, at a conference convened by a resolution of the United Nations General Assembly. Representatives from 110 nations participated, including those from the United States, Great Britain, France, the Soviet Union, and most other United Nations members, as well as several non-members, including Switzerland. The draft was prepared by the International Law Commission. The Convention went into force in January 1980 after ratification by 35 nations. The United States signed but has not yet ratified the Convention; however, the United States considers most of the Vienna Convention's rules as representing customary international law.

Treaties of international peace and cooperation comprise nothing less than the diplomatic landscape of human history: from the benchmark European treaties of the Congress of Vienna (1815), Brest-Litovsk (1918), and Versailles (1919) to the milestone events such as the Covenant of the League of Nations (1919), the United Nations Charter (1948), and the North Atlantic Treaty Organization (1949). Treaties impacting on international peace and disarmament have had surprising durability. The conclusion of the Limited Test Ban Treaty between the United States, the United Kingdom, and the Soviet Union, in 1963, which banned signatories from conducting atmospheric and above-ground nuclear explosions, marked the turning point in the Cold War. The superpowers moved a step closer to nuclear sanity. The 1968 Treaty on the Non-Proliferation of Nuclear Weapons, or NPT, with its 190 signatories, remains the sole global, legal, and diplomatic barrier to the spread of nuclear weapons. The NPT successfully created an international standard against the spread of nuclear weapons, while establishing an international inspection regime that remains the last best hope to prevent the diversion of nuclear reactor fuel to weapons of mass destruction. Diplomacy and diplomats are today the keys to resolving the greatest challenges of the 21st century, including nuclear proliferation (Iran and North Korea, for openers), international terrorism, and global warming, often touching outside the zero-sum game of inter-state competition.

Chapter 2
Diplomacy of the American Revolution

With the conclusion of the Seven Years War in 1763, Great Britain commanded the greatest empire since the fall of Rome. Victory, however, brought with it the necessity of reorganizing the vast North American territories wrested from France and Spain. In an effort to prevent further warfare with the Indian peoples, the Proclamation of 1763 closed the vast trans-Appalachian area to white settlement. With a view to defending and policing these new territories, the British government maintained an unprecedented standing army in mainland America. To meet the costs of this commitment, as well as to relieve the massive financial burden left by the war, London sought to impose new taxes and enforce imperial trade laws that had long been ignored by the colonists. The end of the French and Indian War – as the Seven Years War was known in America – thus marked the end of the period of so-called 'salutary neglect'.

British measures were designed not only to bring peace and stability to North America, but also to require the colonies to share the cost of imperial defence and administration. The colonies, however, had come to think of themselves as self-governing entities, as having 'dominion status', to use a term of later origin, and they refused to have their duties prescribed for them by parliament and king. Parliament and king were unwilling to accept such a novel theory of empire. Great Britain, consequently, found itself involved in a war, not only with its colonies, but eventually with most of Europe. The war, though not wholly disastrous to British arms, deprived Great Britain of the most valuable of its colonial possessions and cast it down from the pinnacle of power that the country had attained by the Peace of Paris of 1763.

The initial aim of armed revolt was not independence, but rather a restoration and recognition of what the colonials held to be their rights as British subjects. They professed to have been content with their status under British policy prior to 1763. That the colonies turned to independence in the second year of the struggle was partly the consequence of the British government's rejection of compromise and its adoption, instead, of severe repressive measures. It was also the consequence of a dawning realization of the advantages that might accrue from independence. No one set forth the arguments for independence so persuasively as a recent immigrant from England named Thomas Paine. Paine had arrived in America in late 1774, leaving behind a number of failed careers. Less than two years later, in January 1776, he published the pamphlet *Common Sense*. This pamphlet sold some 120,000 copies in the first three months, and was the single most effective articulation of the case for independence. Among Paine's arguments, two were significant for the future foreign policy of the United States. Independence, argued Paine, would free the former colonies from being entangled in European wars in which they had no concern. A declaration of independence would also improve their chances of securing foreign aid.

The quest for foreign aid

Greatly inferior to the mother country in numbers, wealth, industry, and military and naval power, the colonies could hardly hope for decisive military success unless aided by one of the major European powers. Months before deciding upon independence, Congress had set up a secret committee to make contact with friends abroad. This committee had sent to Paris a secret agent in the guise of a merchant to seek supplies and credit. The agent, Silas Deane of

Connecticut, arriving in Paris in July 1776, soon found that the French government was disposed to give secret assistance to England's rebelling colonies. French ministers, in fact, had been on the lookout since 1763 for an opportunity to weaken and humiliate France's victorious rival, Great Britain. The celebrated French playwright and amateur diplomat Caron de Beaumarchais, who had already been in contact with another colonial agent, Arthur Lee, in London, believed that such an opportunity had now arrived. So too believed the Comte de Vergennes, French Foreign Minister, and Vergennes and Beaumarchais were able to persuade King Louis XVI that aid to the colonies was in the French interest.

As yet, however, France was not willing to openly avow its friendship for the colonies, and offered material aid only in secret. This was managed through the creation by Beaumarchais of a fictitious commercial firm, Rodrigue Hortalez et Compagnie, through which gunpowder and other essential supplies from the French arsenals were channelled to the armies of George Washington. Spain, too, was persuaded by France to give aid through this and other means. All in all, measured in the dollars of that day, France contributed to the American cause nearly $2,000,000 in subsidies and over $6,350,000 in loans; Spain, approximately $400,000 and $250,000 in subsidies and loans, respectively.

The French alliance

These arrangements for secret 'lend-lease' had been instituted before Deane's arrival in Paris. After the Declaration of Independence, Congress sent to France the most widely known, most admired, and most persuasive American of his day, Benjamin Franklin. In Paris, he joined Deane and Arthur Lee, who had come from London, to form a three-man American commission. The commission's work was severely compromised by enemy agents, leading the historian Jonathon Dull to label it 'virtually an unemployment bureau for the British secret service'. The most important of British agents was Dr Edward Bancroft, a native of

Massachusetts who had been employed as Deane's secretary. Bancroft was secretly in the pay of the British government, to which he faithfully reported the work of the commission and its relations with the French ministers. Arthur Lee was convinced of Bancroft's treachery but could not shake Franklin's and Deane's

2. Benjamin Franklin

faith in their employee. In addition to the presence of enemy agents, Franklin frequently leaked information for political reasons, while Deane used inside information in pursuit of a number of speculative schemes.

The principal purpose of Franklin's mission was to secure from the French government official recognition of the United States as an independent nation. Recognition could be accomplished by the signing of a treaty between France and the United States. Franklin brought with him to Paris a draft of a proposed Treaty of Amity and Commerce, which had been prepared by a committee of Congress and which embodied the liberal commercial principles that Congress hoped to see adopted, not only by France but by the entire trading world. This Plan of Treaties of 1776 was the first major state paper dealing with American foreign policy, and would guide the makers of such policy far beyond the exigencies of the Revolution. John Adams, the principal author of the model treaty, repeatedly asserted that any Franco-American treaty should take the form of a commercial connection with no military or political ties. Adams said of France:

> We ought not to enter into any Alliance with her, which should entangle Us in any future Wars in Europe, . . . We ought to lay it down as a first principle and a Maxim never to be forgotten, to maintain an entire Neutrality in all future European Wars.

Though friendly to the United States, Vergennes was unwilling to grant formal recognition, thus risking war with England, until the Americans could offer some evidence of their ability to do their share in winning the war. Quite understandably, he did not wish to involve France in a war for a losing cause. Such evidence was not forthcoming until December 1777, when news arrived that General Burgoyne's British army, thrusting down from Montreal into New York, had been forced to surrender to General Gates at Saratoga. This was what Vergennes had been waiting for; he tried to enlist Spain in the cause, and when Spain procrastinated, resolved that France should proceed without it.

On 17 December, the American commissioners were informed that France would grant recognition and make a treaty with the United States. On 6 February 1778, a Treaty of Amity and Commerce and a Treaty of Alliance were signed in Paris, the latter to take effect if Great Britain went to war with France because of the former. The Treaty of Amity and Commerce clearly reflected the principles set down by Adams in the Plan of Treaties of 1776. The Treaty of Alliance, however, ran contrary to his calls to avoid an alliance with France 'which might embarrass Us in after times and involve Us in future European Wars'.

Vergennes had hastened to take this action out of fear that England would effect a reconciliation with its former colonies. Burgoyne's surrender had produced a sensation in England and led the ministry to offer liberal terms of settlement to the Americans. In March, Parliament passed a series of bills repealing all the legislation enacted since 1763 of which the colonists had complained. In April, a commission headed by the Earl of Carlisle was dispatched to America, empowered to offer Congress virtually everything it had claimed, independence alone excepted, if the former colonies would lay down their arms and resume their allegiance to the British Crown. The right to control their own taxation, to elect their governors and other officials formerly appointed, to be represented in Parliament if they so desired, to continue Congress as an American legislature, release from quitrents (rent paid in lieu of required feudal services), assurance that their colonial charters would not be altered without their consent, and full pardon for all who had engaged in rebellion – these terms of the offer indicate how far Great Britain was willing to go to save its empire from disruption. In effect, it was offering 'dominion status' to America.

Had such an offer been made at any time prior to the Declaration of Independence, perhaps at any time prior to Burgoyne's surrender, it may well have been accepted, and the troublesome thirteen states would have become the first British dominion. The offer came too late. With recognition and the promise of an alliance and open aid from France, independence seemed assured, and there was no turning back. Congress ratified the treaties with France without even stopping to parley with the Carlisle Commission.

The Treaty of Amity and Commerce placed each nation on a most-favoured-nation basis with reference to the other and embodied, practically unaltered, the liberal principles of the 'Plan of 1776' – principles which would protect the interest of either signatory that might chance to be neutral when the other was at war. The Treaty of Alliance was to go into effect if France should become embroiled in the existing war against Great Britain. Its object was 'to maintain effectually the liberty, Sovereignty, and independence absolute and unlimited' of the United States. France renounced forever any designs upon Bermuda or upon any parts of the continent of North America which before the Treaty of Paris of 1763 or by virtue of that treaty had belonged to Great Britain or the former British colonies. It reserved the right to possess itself of any of the British West Indian colonies. The United States, on the other hand, was free to conquer and hold Bermuda or any of Great Britain's mainland possessions. Neither party was to make a separate peace with Great Britain nor lay down its arms until American independence was won. Both parties mutually guaranteed 'from the present time and forever against all other powers' the American possessions which they then held and with which they might emerge from the war. France, in addition, undertook to guarantee the liberty, sovereignty, and independence of the United States.

The treaty just described constituted the only 'entangling alliance' in which the United States participated until the middle of the 20th century. And it was to cause serious embarrassment before it was set aside in 1800, but in the winning of independence, it was indispensable. A French army under General Rochambeau was sent to America, and French fleets under Admirals d'Estaing and de Grasse operated off the American coast. The importance of French aid is illustrated by the fact that in the final scene of the Revolution, at Yorktown, Cornwallis's British army was caught between a French fleet and an allied army, of which two-thirds were French.

Spain and the Revolution

Spain, though bound to France by a dynastic alliance, the 'Family Compact', and though giving secret aid to the United States, hung back from entering the war for over a year after France became a belligerent. There were advantages that Spain might gain from a successful war with England, namely the recovery of Gibraltar (lost in 1713) and of Florida (lost in 1763). Gibraltar, the more valuable of these, the Spanish court hoped to regain peaceably, as a reward for mediating between Great Britain and France. Only when Great Britain declined the proffered service did Spain sign a definite alliance with France – the Convention of Aranjuez, 12 April 1779 – and declare war against Great Britain, on 21 June 1779. The Franco-American Treaty of Alliance had reserved for Spain the right to become a member, but Spain declined to sign it or to make any kind of treaty with the United States. A colonial power itself, Spain naturally hesitated to give formal acknowledgement to a rebellion of the colonies of Great Britain. John Jay spent many bitter months in Madrid asking in vain for recognition. Even an offer to waive the American claim of right to navigate the Mississippi River could not persuade the Spanish government to recognize the young republic. By the Convention of Aranjuez, France and Spain agreed that neither would make peace until Spain had recovered Gibraltar. Since the United States had promised not to make peace without France, it could not, if all treaty engagements were observed, make peace till Gibraltar was restored to Spain.

In America, Spanish interests ran counter to those of the United States. The United States desired the Mississippi River as its western boundary and the right of navigating the river through Spanish territory to the Gulf of Mexico. Spain, anxious to monopolize as far as possible the navigation and commerce of both river and gulf, was unwilling to concede to the Americans either the use of the river or a foothold on its eastern bank. If the Spanish had their way, the western boundary of the United States would be fixed as near as possible to the summit of the Appalachians.

The bargaining position of Spain was strengthened by the daring and vigour of Bernardo de Galvez, the young governor of Louisiana. Less than two years after Spain's entry into the war, he had routed the British out of all of West Florida, from Natchez on the north, to Pensacola on the east. He established Spain's claim to a cession of Florida at the end of the war and to full control of the lower Mississippi.

A pawn in the European chess game

In order to win independence, the United States had found it necessary to involve itself in the international rivalries and politics of Europe. Those same rivalries and politics, however, threatened to terminate the war with American independence still unwon. Spain, having entered the war reluctantly, soon grew tired of it. In 1780, the Spanish government received a British mission, come to discuss peace terms. For America, the Spanish ministers proposed a long truce between Great Britain and its 'colonies', without specific recognition of independence and with a division of territory on the basis of *uti possidetis*, or retention by each party of the areas then occupied. This would have left the British in control of Maine, the northern frontier, New York City, Long Island, and the principal seaports south of Virginia.

Vergennes disapproved of these Anglo-Spanish conversations, which violated the Convention of Aranjuez. He was willing to listen, however, to proposals for mediation from the Czarina Catherine II of Russia and the Austrian Emperor, Joseph II, which would have had much the same effect in America. John Adams, who had been named American peace commissioner and came from the Hague to Paris at Vergennes' behest, rejected the proposal out of hand when Vergennes laid it before him. No truce, he said, till all British troops were withdrawn from the United States; no negotiation with England without guarantees that American sovereignty and independence would be respected. But in America, Congress was more easily persuaded than was Adams. Under pressure (and in some instances monetary persuasion) from La Luzerne, the French minister, Congress, on 15 June 1781, drew up new instructions to its prospective peace commissioners in Europe. Not only were they directed to accept the mediation of the Czarina and the Emperor; they were to place themselves in the hands of the French ministers, 'to undertake nothing in the negotiations for peace or truce without their knowledge and concurrence', and ultimately to be governed 'by their advice and opinion'. It was perhaps fortunate for the United States that the British government rejected the proposal for mediation.

Great Britain in difficulty

The surrender of Cornwallis to Washington and Rochambeau at Yorktown, 19 October 1781, was the climax of Great Britain's misfortunes. The country was now at war, or on the verge of war, with most of the Western world. To the list of its open enemies, Great Britain had itself added the Netherlands, forcing the Dutch into war rather than permit continuance of their neutral trade with France. The Baltic countries, Russia, Denmark, and Sweden, had in 1780 organized themselves into a League of Armed Neutrality for the purpose of protecting their commerce against what they considered the illegitimate exactions of the British navy; and they had been joined by Prussia, the Emperor (of the Holy Roman Empire), the Kingdom of the Two Sicilies, and even Portugal, Great Britain's traditional ally. There was little that the British could hope to gain by prolonging the war.

In February 1782, following receipt of the news of the disaster at Yorktown, the British House of Commons resolved that the war ought to be terminated. In March, the ministry of Lord North, whose policies had precipitated the American conflict, resigned, and a new ministry headed by the Marquis of Rockingham took office. The Earl of Shelburne, as Secretary of State for the Southern Department, initiated peace talks by sending Richard Oswald, a Scot, to confer with the American representatives in Paris. After Rockingham's death in July 1782, Shelburne became Prime Minister but continued to guide negotiations with the United States. This was fortunate, for Shelburne was an advocate of a generous peace, which might result in recapturing for Great Britain the bulk of American trade and, at some future date, perhaps, tempt the United States back into some sort of imperial federation.

The American Congress named five peace commissioners, of whom three actually handled the negotiations. Franklin was in Paris when the talks began. John Jay, who had been vainly seeking recognition and a treaty in Madrid, arrived in June 1782. John Adams, who had secured recognition and a loan from the Netherlands, reached Paris in October. Henry Laurens was on hand in time to sign the treaty. Thomas Jefferson, the fifth of those named by Congress, declined to serve. Most of the work was done by Franklin and Jay, with Adams giving valuable aid towards the close of the negotiations.

The stakes of diplomacy

The American commissioners had three principal objectives: (1) recognition of independence, which was now assured; (2) the widest boundaries obtainable; (3) retention of the inshore fishing privileges on the coasts of British North America that the colonials had enjoyed as British subjects. The British government was ready to recognize American independence and to act generously on the other American demands. It hoped in turn to secure from the United States: (1) provision for the payment of the pre-revolutionary debts of American planters and others to British creditors; and (2) an agreement to compensate the Loyalists (Americans who had sided with Great Britain in the struggle) for the lands and other property that had been seized by the states in which they lived.

Of the American demands, the most controversial was that concerning boundaries, for American claims on this point involved not only adjustments with Great Britain, but also disputes with Spain – disputes in which Vergennes chose to support his Spanish rather than his American ally. In their more sanguine moments, Benjamin Franklin and other American leaders dreamed of including in their confederacy the whole of British North America and certain outlying islands. Such hopes had no chance of fulfilment. What the United States Congress laid claim to as a matter of right was the entire western country between the Appalachian Mountains and the Mississippi River, extending from the 31st parallel on the south to a northern line drawn from the St Lawrence River at north latitude 45° to Lake Nipissing (the south-western boundary of Quebec before 1774) and thence to the source of the Mississippi. These claims, based chiefly upon the sea-to-sea clauses in certain colonial charters, had never been taken seriously by the British government, which in the years since 1763 had acted upon the theory that the western lands still belonged to the Crown.

South of the Ohio River, American settlements in central Kentucky and eastern and central Tennessee gave the United States a solid basis for claiming those areas, but farther south it was the Spanish, not the Americans, who had driven the British out. The Spanish held the east bank of the Mississippi as far north as Natchez. They hoped, as was previously noted, to deny the Americans access to the Mississippi and to draw the boundary as near as possible to the Appalachian watershed. In this endeavour they had French support.

In the summer of 1779, Congress had taken the first step towards peace negotiations by naming John Adams commissioner for that purpose. In instructions prepared for him on 14 August 1779, it proposed boundaries including the entire area claimed by the states from the mountains to the Mississippi. It added that although it was 'of the utmost importance to the peace and Commerce of the United States that Canada and Nova Scotia should be ceded', and that equal rights in the fisheries should be guaranteed, a desire to terminate the war had led Congress to refrain from making the acquisition of these objects an ultimatum. Subsequently, under stress of military necessity and pressure from the French minister, Congress modified those demands. In the new instructions of 15 June 1781, it insisted only upon independence and the preservation of the treaties with France as indispensable conditions. With regard to boundaries, the commissioners were to regard the earlier instructions as indicating 'the desires and expectations of Congress', but were not to adhere to them if they presented an obstacle to peace. The task of the commissioners was to get as much as they could of the terms proposed two years earlier. In this respect, they were quite successful.

The peace negotiations

The first obstacles encountered by the Americans were erected by the Spanish and French, not by the British. When John Jay arrived in Paris, suspicious of both Spain and France after his futile mission in Madrid, he found disturbing confirmation of his distrust. Conversations with the Spanish ambassador in Paris and with a spokesman for Vergennes showed that the Spanish, with French support, were bent upon excluding the United States from the Mississippi Valley. French support of Spanish claims impaired the confidential relations between Vergennes and the American commissioners. Vergennes had previously agreed that the American and French negotiations should proceed separately but at equal pace and with the understanding that neither settlement should become effective without the other. Franklin and Jay now proceeded to negotiate their own preliminary terms with the British, neglecting, with considerable justification, to make those 'most candid and confidential communications' to the French ministers enjoined upon them by their instructions of 15 June 1781. In negotiating their settlement with Great Britain, they simply disregarded Spanish claims in the western country north of the 31st parallel, assuming (as did the British) that that country was still Great Britain's to dispose of.

In informal talks with Oswald, Franklin had already sketched what, as an American, he considered the 'necessary' and the 'advisable' terms of a lasting peace. Among 'necessary' terms he included, after independence and withdrawal of troops, 'a confinement of the boundaries of Canada' to what they had been before the Quebec Act (that is, the St Lawrence–Nipissing line), 'if not to a still more contracted state', and the retention of fishing privileges. Among 'advisable' terms which might be expected to contribute to a permanent reconciliation, he mentioned indemnification by Great Britain of those persons who had been ruined through the devastations of war, acknowledgement of error expressed in an Act of Parliament or in some other public document, admission of American ships and trade to British and Irish ports upon the same terms as those of Britain, and 'giving up every part of Canada'.

A delay in the negotiations now ensued, first because Oswald had no formal commission as an agent of the British government, and after his commission arrived on 8 August, because it failed to authorize him to recognize the independence of the United States as preliminary to negotiation but, on the contrary, empowered him to treat with representatives of 'colonies' of Great Britain. It did, however, authorize him to make recognition of independence the first article of the proposed treaty. Franklin and Jay were at first inclined to insist upon formal recognition of independence as a condition precedent to negotiation; but, becoming alarmed lest France use any further delay to their disadvantage, they agreed to accept as recognition a new commission that authorized Oswald to treat with commissioners of the United States of America. In this meticulous stickling for matters of form, and with the passage of time, the situation was modified to the disadvantage of the United States.

On 1 September, instructions were sent to Oswald to agree to terms of peace on the basis of the 'necessary' terms proposed by Franklin, conceding to the United States the western country as far north as the Nipissing line, and making no stipulation for the payment of pre-war debts or the restitution of property confiscated from the Loyalists. A draft of a treaty on these terms was actually initialled by the commissioners on 5 October and referred to London. The unfortunate results of delay now became apparent. News had arrived in London of the failure of a major assault upon Gibraltar, which had been besieged for three years by Spanish and French land and sea forces. With this victory in hand, Shelburne took a firmer tone towards the United States. He not only insisted that something be done for creditors and Loyalists, but made a last-moment attempt to hold the north-west, though this latter move may have been merely a gesture designed to secure concessions on the other points. 'They wanted', Franklin reported, 'to bring their boundary down to the Ohio and to settle the loyalists in the Illinois country. We did not choose such neighbors.'

The Americans, now reinforced by Adams, insisted upon retention of the north-west, but were ready to make concessions on this and other points. They agreed to inclusion in the treaty of articles in the interest of the Loyalists and the British creditors. They accepted the St Croix River instead of the St John, which Congress had originally proposed, as the north-eastern boundary, thereby laying the basis of a controversy which took 60 years to settle. In the west, they dropped the Nipissing line proposal, agreeing to accept instead either of two alternatives: a line drawn due west along the 45th parallel from the St Lawrence to the Mississippi, or a line through the middle of the St Lawrence and the Great Lakes and thence via the Lake of the Woods to the Mississippi. The British accepted the second alternative. The preliminary treaty was signed at Paris on 30 November 1782, not to become effective until France also made peace with England.

The treaty thus signed and, in due course, ratified by the parties was less favourable to the United States in three respects than the draft initialled on 5 October. It contained troublesome provisions for Loyalists and for British creditors, and the northern boundary

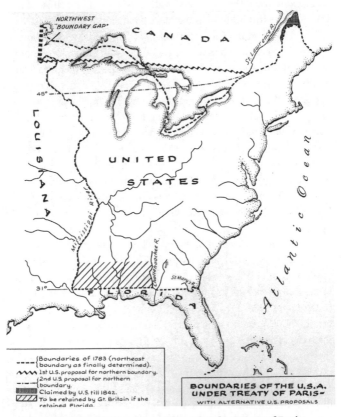

3. Map of the boundaries of the USA under the Treaty of Paris

followed the river and lake line instead of that by way of Lake Nipissing. By the latter change, the United States lost the greater and the most valuable part of the modern province of Ontario. Had Jay and Franklin been willing to treat with Oswald on the basis of his first commission, it is at least possible that they might have agreed upon Franklin's 'necessary terms' early in September, instead of a month later, and that Shelburne might have accepted these terms before he received news of the victory at Gibraltar.

What is remarkable about the treaty is that the United States got as much as it did, especially that the British surrendered title to all territory east of the Mississippi between the Great Lakes and the 31st parallel. For the explanation of this surrender, one must look neither to the legal weight of the colonial charters, nor to the military victories of George Rogers Clark, but to the enlightened policy of the Earl of Shelburne. Desirous of a peace of reconciliation, he saw a means of achieving it at small cost to the empire. The north-west, demanded by the Americans, appeared to him to be of slight value to Great Britain. The regulation of the fur trade in that area was proving ruinously expensive to the royal treasury, and experience had seemed to show that the region was of little value without control of the mouth of the Mississippi, now more firmly than ever in the hands of Spain. Why not buy American good will at so cheap a price?

The treaty

In detail, the principal provisions of the preliminary treaty signed on 30 November 1782 were as follows. The boundary of the United States began at the mouth of the St Croix River on the Maine frontier, followed that river to its source, and thence ran due north to the highlands dividing the St Lawrence from the Atlantic watershed, along those highlands to the north-westernmost head of the Connecticut River, and down that river to the 45th parallel, which it followed to the St Lawrence. It then followed the middle of the St Lawrence and of Lakes Ontario, Erie, and Huron, and connecting waters to Lake Superior; through that lake to Long Lake and then through certain small lakes and streams to the Lake of the Woods, from the north-westernmost point of which it was to be drawn due west to the Mississippi – an impossible line, since the Mississippi rose well to the southward. It followed the Mississippi down to the 31st parallel, ran due east along that parallel to the Chattahoochee, descended that stream to its junction with the Flint, leaped thence straight to the head of the St Mary's River, which it followed to the Atlantic. A secret article, introduced by the British but not incorporated in the final treaty, stipulated that if Great Britain retained West Florida, the northern line of that province should be, as it had been since 1764, not the 31st parallel but a line drawn east from the junction of the Yazoo with the Mississippi. The navigation of the Mississippi was to remain forever 'free and open to the subjects of Great Britain, and the citizens of the United States'.

Great Britain acknowledged the independence and sovereignty of the thirteen states individually, promised to withdraw all its armies, garrisons, and fleets from their soil and waters 'with all convenient speed', and conceded to American fishermen the 'liberty' to ply their trade much as before in the territorial waters of British North America. The United States, on its part, made certain promises in the interest of Loyalists and British creditors. The parties agreed that creditors on either side should 'meet with no lawful impediment' in the recovery of the full value of *bona fide* debts previously contracted. The United States agreed that there should be no further prosecutions or confiscations of property against any persons for the parts they had taken in the war, and promised that it would 'earnestly recommend' to the legislatures of the states that, with certain exceptions, rights and properties of Loyalists be restored.

This preliminary treaty, minus the secret article, became the definitive treaty, signed 3 September 1783, at the same time that Great Britain made peace with its other enemies. Great Britain ceded the Floridas, with limits undefined, to Spain, which was not a party to the treaty between Great Britain and the United States, and hence did not consider itself bound by its provisions with respect to the navigation of the Mississippi and the southern boundary of the United States. With both Spain and Great Britain, the United States still had many difficulties to overcome before the paper stipulations of the treaty could be converted into reality.

Problems of independence

Americans soon learned that independence was no bed of roses. When the war officially ended in 1783, the new government had been recognized by France, Great Britain, the Netherlands, and Sweden. Inexperienced diplomats from the United States had wandered over Europe in vain efforts to secure recognition from Russia, Prussia, Austria, Spain, and the Grand Duke of Tuscany. In all these courts they had been coldly received. Few monarchs cared to imitate the indiscretion of Louis XVI of France, by countenancing rebellion and the institution of republican government.

A few other recognitions followed independence. In 1784, Spain finally gave in, sending Don Diego de Gardoqui as its first minister to the United States. Prussia made a treaty in 1785; Morocco in 1786. By 1787, then, the United States had commercial treaties with those two powers and with France (1778), the Netherlands (1782), and Sweden (1783). It had no commercial treaty with Great Britain until 1794; no treaty at all with Spain until 1795. The British government thought so little of the importance of the United States that, though it received John Adams as minister in 1785 and maintained consular or other agents in American ports, it did not send a fully fledged minister to Philadelphia until 1791.

There were reasons for this temporary 'underprivileged' status of the United States. It was an upstart nation, the product of revolution, an experiment in democracy, small in population and poor in fluid resources. But it also, under the Articles of

Confederation, had a government that no foreign power need respect – a government without dependable revenue, without an army or navy, and without power to coerce the governments of the thirteen individual states. Such a government was unable to fulfil its obligations under the Treaty of Peace. Such a government could not make promises with assurance that they would be observed, or threats with any expectation that they would be carried out. Such a government was incapable of securing equality of commercial treatment abroad. It was incapable of enforcing its sovereignty in the area assigned to it by the Treaty of Peace or of putting an end, by either diplomacy or force, to foreign occupation of its soil. Not until after it was replaced by the more effective government provided for by the Constitution of 1787 were any of the pressing national problems solved. Even then, their solution owed much to the involvement of France, Spain, and Great Britain in the wars of the French Revolution. Then, to quote the familiar aphorism of Professor Samuel F. Bemis, 'Europe's distress became America's advantage'.

Chapter 3
Diplomatic origins of the Great War and Versailles

Sometimes it is difficult to believe, but the fifteen years before the outbreak of World War I witnessed the heyday of the international peace movement. International peace societies became affluent and respectable, the Permanent Court of Arbitration was established at The Hague, and conciliation treaties were concluded in dozen lots. Some who lived through those calm and peaceful years believed, in all seriousness, that the days of war – at least major war – were in the past. It seemed clear that given the costly and destructive potentialities of modern technology, even victors in such a struggle would lose far more than they could possibly gain. Humankind, it was assumed, was a rational being and could see the folly of squandering precious resources in a game of self-destruction. Complaining of the costly European arms race of the era, German Social Democrat Eduard Bernstein wrote in 1893 that 'This continued arming, compelling the others to keep up with Germany, is a kind of warfare. I do not know whether this expression has been used previously, but one could say it is a cold war. . . . There is no shooting, but there is bleeding', in the sense of undermining the welfare of the peoples and the squandering of the resources needed in the work of social reform. Many thoughtful people had doubtless reached the same conclusion as British writer Norman Angel whose influential book, *The Great Illusion*, published in 1910, made a compelling case that no one really wins a modern war.

That all changed in the Bosnian capital of Sarajevo on 28 June 1914, when an assassination ignited a diplomatic crisis that culminated in a major world war. Gavrilo Princip, a young, ardent Serbian nationalist and member of a terrorist group, the Black Hand, mortally wounded Archduke Francis Ferdinand, heir to the Austro-Hungarian throne, and his beloved wife Sophie. Since there was good reason to suspect Serbian involvement, the Austrian government decided to resolve the Balkan problem with violence, ending once and for all the constant threat to the stability of the multi-national Hapsburg Empire. This was an area of vital interest to the Hapsburgs, because they feared unrest among their own Slavic population as well as Russian expansion. The Vienna government sent a legal expert to the scene to collect evidence in order to prepare a tight case. In July, the teenaged Princip and his fellow conspirators were placed on trial and were found guilty. When Belgrade failed to comply with Vienna's subsequent demands, Austria-Hungary declared war against Serbia on 28 July, and Belgrade was bombarded the next day.

Diplomatic origins of World War I

Because of Europe's rival alliances and age-old ambitions and passions, the Great Powers soon found themselves engulfed in war, the veritable tidal wave produced by nationalism, imperialism, and militarism. Within days of Austria-Hungary's declaration of war, Imperial Germany (the other half of the Central Powers) declared war on Tsarist Russia, after the latter began general mobilization to defend Serbia; Germany declared war on France, after anticipating French support of Russia; and Great Britain declared war on Germany, after the German invasion of Belgium, whose neutrality Britain had long guaranteed. Japan came in as Britain's ally in the Far East, and Italy joined France and its allies (the Entente, or Allied Powers). Eventually two dozen nations, including Turkey, Bulgaria, Romania, Greece, and, finally, America, in 1917, became immersed in the great struggle. German chancellor Otto von Bismarck's prediction that 'some damned foolish thing' in the Balkans would one day set off a general European war had proved correct. British statesman Sir Edward Grey also got it right when he said 'the lights are going out all over Europe, they will not be lit again in our lifetime'. He might just as well have included the next generation, as the events of 1914 paved the way for the next war, one continuous war, a new terrible Thirty Years War.

But it would be wrong, however, to imagine that World War I, which resulted in the most extensive cultural devastation and mass killing in Europe since the Thirty Years War, was caused by a single assassination. Rather, its origins lay principally, though not exclusively, in the alliance diplomacy that had over many years developed between Germany, Austria, and Italy, on the one hand, and France and Russia, on the other. It was the entangling alliances that created the house of cards that when war broke out, or for that matter when the Russian Empire declared mobilization of its armies, collapsed, and the Great Powers – minus Italy, which held out for the highest bidder – went to war. The key to understanding this process – and German mentality on the eve of World War I – necessarily begins with the rise of Prussia-Germany to Great Power status in the 19th century.

The unique role of the German officer corps

When one looks back over the history of the rise of Prussia-Germany to Great Power status in the 19th century, one sees that the achievement of the unification under Prussia was the consequence of three well-planned, short, sharp so-called cabinet wars (*Kabinettskriege*) designed and executed for very specific and limited aims. These were certainly not wars of conquest, but rather for discrete political objectives, planned by the political leadership and carried out by highly professional generals. Behind these 19th-century achievements was the remarkable history of the rise of Prussia to European power status under the Hohenzollern Electors and kings in the 17th and 18th centuries. It was they,

4. Trench warfare: *Oppy Wood* (1917), by John Nash

particularly the King of Prussia from 1740 to 1786, Frederick the Great, who established the tradition of Prussian-German statecraft that rested on the correct relationship between the political leadership and the generals who served. This meant essentially that the king was responsible for all policy, and that if he decided that a war was necessary, for reasons of state, he commissioned the military to plan and execute it. In this way, it was understood that the maximum security of the country could be secured. At all important levels, then, the Hohenzollern dynasty exerted a shaping influence on the formation of Prussian-German political culture that lasted until the end of World War II.

It should also be kept in mind that in a land-locked country like Prussia-Germany, with potential enemies on all sides,

German statesmen would always have to reckon with the possibility of war at any time, and a permanent threat of attack, perhaps not tomorrow, but certainly some time in the future. Given that situation, the technical proficiency of the German officer corps was given the highest priority. Indeed, in Prussia-Germany, after the unification in 1871, one can observe a process evolving whereby the foreign policy priorities were governed by the army, which in the end came to dominate diplomacy.

The fateful permanence of Franco-German enmity

When German Chancellor Otto von Bismarck founded the Reich in 1871, it was mainly at the expense of France in the third war of unification. France had been brutally humiliated, the emperor having been captured and sent into exile, the country suffering partial occupation, a massive war indemnity, and the loss of a major province, Alsace-Lorraine, which became a so-called *Reichsland* until the French retrieved it after World War I. Such national shame meant that France had been turned into a permanent enemy of the new German Empire, and, as a consequence, one had to expect it would want revenge. Bismarck was acutely aware of this, and designed his diplomacy from that time forward on the assumption that France would always want to join with another major European power to keep Germany at bay and, at the right moment, to attack.

Much of the diplomatic history of this period at first revolves around this historic enmity between France and Germany and, specifically, over Alsace-Lorraine. And one can debate, as historians have, to what extent revenge permeated the ranks of French society. If it had been possible to ask people who France would go to war against – if they had polls in those days – most people would probably have said England, not Germany. But the spectre of that enmity was always there for Bismarck. Politically, then, the German chancellor had to head off the nightmare

5. Prince Otto von Bismarck

coalition against Germany, namely, France and Russia. Fearful
of being attacked from both the east and west by France and
Russia, the entire thrust of Bismarck's diplomacy was to
maintain alliances as long as possible to delay the inevitable – the
next war that was bound to happen sooner or later. Bismarck's
concept was always to be '*a trios*', to be three – always in a group
of three powers aligned against France or, put another way, if

there are five you want to be three. But there were basically two potential free agents: Italy, which would go to the highest bidder in 1915, and Great Britain. Nor was it a given that Great Britain would ally with France, its great enemy for centuries, or ally with Russia, because Great Britain and Russia had been fighting for a very long time in the 'Great Game', for control along places such as northern India, Pakistan, and all the way into South Asia.

In 1873, Bismarck cobbled together a pact between the three emperors of East/Central Europe: Prussia-Germany, Austria-Hungary, and Tsarist Russia. Concluded during a visit of the German chancellor to St Petersburg, the pact provided that if either party were attacked by another European power, the other would come to its assistance with 200,000 men. In short, Bismarck was trying to find a way to have two reliable friends. But this was going to prove extraordinarily difficult in the long term. Russia, especially, was not fully at ease with the arrangement. So, in 1879, Bismarck forged another kind of alliance between Germany and Austria-Hungary. Directed squarely against Russia, the Dual Alliance was predicated on German support for Austria-Hungary and Hungarian resistance against Russian activities in the Balkans. Concluded for five years, but regularly renewed, it remained in force until 1918 and was the foundation stone of Bismarck's alliance system. The provisions were unequivocal: if either party were attacked by Russia, the other should come to its assistance with all forces; if either should be attacked by some other power, its partner should preserve at least neutrality; and if some other power should be supported by Russia, then each ally was obliged to aid the other. The Dual Alliance remained one of the continuities of the entire period, and explains why it was in July 1914 that the Germans gave the famous blank cheque to the Austrians after the assassination of Francis Ferdinand, allowing Vienna to do whatever it wanted to Serbia, knowing full well that it would eventually involve going to war with Russia.

The Reinsurance Treaty

As European politics developed in the 1890s, it was becoming increasingly clear that Bismarck's objective to sustain a reliable alignment of three powers was really not attainable, simply because the vital interests of Russia and Austria-Hungary could not be reconciled for long enough, particularly in the Balkans, which was perennially a source of friction and conflict. Bismarck then tried to stitch up one last deal with Russia in order to keep it in line with a separate and secret treaty called the Reinsurance Treaty in 1887, to replace the expiring Alliance of the Three Emperors (1881), which Russia refused to renew. Essentially, the two powers promised each other neutrality in the event of either becoming involved in war with a third power, but this was not to apply in case of *aggressive* war against France, or of Russia against Austria. They also were to work for the maintenance of the *status quo* in the Balkans, with Germany recognizing Russia's preponderant influence in Bulgaria. This famous treaty represented Bismarck's last effort to keep Russia from France and to buy its friendship by signing away things that he knew Russia could never get on account of Austrian opposition. But this proved unworkable, and the treaty lapsed formally after the German chancellor was retired in 1891.

It had fairly much become a dead letter before that. German historians have often tried to portray the Reinsurance Treaty as Bismarck's most brilliant concept because if it could have been kept alive, then France and Russia could not have entered into the military alliance they did in 1893. At that time, there was an exchange of notes between the Russian and French governments, formally accepting a military convention worked out 18 months before. The agreement was really political as much as military, but classed as a military convention in order to circumvent the French constitution, which required submission of treaties to the chamber of deputies. The convention was to remain in force as long as the Triple Alliance (1892). It provided: that if France were attacked by

Germany, or by Italy supported by Germany, Russia would supply all available forces against Germany; if Russia were attacked by Germany, or by Italy supported by Germany, France would supply all available forces against Germany. Moreover, and more ominously, in case the forces of the Triple Alliance, or of any one power member to it (Germany, Austria, and Italy), mobilized, France and Russia should mobilize without delay. While formal alliances were not published in *Figaro* or in *Le Temps*, or any other newspaper, everybody knew the rough outlines of the pact. The foreign ministries in London, in Vienna, in Berlin knew enough to know what the treaty meant: the diplomatic isolation of France had ended and Bismarck's nightmare had become a reality.

The militarization of German diplomacy

In the post-Bismarck era of diplomacy, the Prussian-German general staff felt obliged from now on to prioritize the military solution to their diplomatic dilemma. They had already foreseen the eventuality of having to fight a two-front war against France in the west and Russia in the east, and had placed emphasis on strong defences there, that is, in the east. However, under the new chief of the general staff, Count von Schlieffen, from 1891 to 1905, a revolutionary new concept took over, and it is important to dwell on it for a moment for what it reveals about the relationship between the military and the civilian government in the German Empire. The first thing to keep in mind is that German leadership believed in the inevitability of war with France, and whoever its allies might be. That was the only scenario they could imagine. Then, von Schlieffen came along and realized that the war would definitely have to be fought on two fronts, against France and Russia simultaneously. This posed a fundamental problem of logistics, but von Schlieffen had a solution to the problem. It was based on a new concept – new for the modern era, anyway – called the 'war of annihilation' (*der Vernchtungskrieg*). How was it supposed to work? Because Russia was so big and unwieldy and would take a long time to mobilize in the east, there would be a brief opportunity to destroy France, first in a lightning war (*Blitzkrieg*) that would be over in a few weeks, as in 1870, and then, having annihilated the French army, the German army could be turned eastward to bring the smaller holding army against Russia up to full strength in that sector. Superior German armament and planning would take care of the lumbering Russians in time for everybody to be home for Christmas. The concept bequeathed by von Schlieffen militarized German diplomacy even further.

What seems incredible, from today's standpoint, was that the civilian leadership, that is, the chancellor and the cabinet, was not informed of crucial details. The most important one was that the plan in the west required the German army to march through neutral Belgium in order to be able as quickly as possible to get into position north of Paris to lay siege to the city. Another German army was simultaneously to drive across the Rhine, in the south, and envelop Paris from that direction. As stressed, it was meant to be over in two weeks, a 'super-Cannae', as von Schlieffen called it, in an allusion to the annihilation of Roman troops by Hannibal in 216 BC. And it nearly worked. So what frustrated it? For one thing, Belgium refused to roll over, rejecting German demands that its armies be allowed to march through Belgium; indeed, the Belgium army fought bravely, even heroically, against overpowering military strength and savagery, including the summary execution of thousands of civilians as well as the calculated spoliation of the famous library of Louvain university and other historical sites. For another, and more important, the Schlieffen plan took no real account of the intervention of the British on behalf of Belgium, with whom they had a treaty dating from 1839 (the London Protocol). To be sure, von Schlieffen may have considered a British intervention, but he regarded it as a mere irritation, as though London could ever tolerate Belgium occupied by a potentially very hostile power. In his mind, the British could not fight a land war, a notion gleaned by their apparent dismal performance against the Boers in the South African War (1899–1902).

Looking back, one would have to say that von Schlieffen was at the very least basing his assessments on prejudice, because what actually frustrated his finely tuned timetable from working out was the intervention of the British Expeditionary Force. The British ability to shoot rapid fire, a hard lesson learned as a consequence of initial poor performance against the Boers, held up the German army, poised as it was in September 1914 to encircle Paris. The simple conclusion was that the decision to march through Belgium automatically involved Britain in the war on the side of France, and this fact resulted in the otherwise brilliant Schlieffen plan collapsing. But the point to remember is that it was both politically and militarily flawed to start with. After the war, in his memoirs, the German Chancellor Bethmann-Hollweg admitted as much. In fact, when he learned that the plan would set the British in motion, his nerve was effectively broken and the real government of Germany devolved into the hand of the military.

The irrational continuation of the war of annihilation

Now that the plan failed, the new commanding officer Erich von Falkenhayn, who replaced the younger von Moltke, believed, or rather pretended to believe, he could still reach the original objective in the west and east, but the resources in men and materiel were simply not up to the gigantic task. Von Falkenhayn was really not himself totally certain he could bring it off. In early August, at the beginning of hostilities, he wrote: 'If in this undertaking we should be defeated, it was still a wonderful thing.' Expressed alternatively, he went on: 'We feel obliged to go through with this even though it will probably end in disaster.'

But it just got worse. Von Falkenhayn told the chancellor on 18 November 1914: 'So long as Russia, France and England hold together it will be impossible for us to bring off victory.' Indeed, von Falkenhayn would have preferred to make a separate peace with each of them, but he appreciated it was ruled out by the

London Treaty of September 1914 that obliged the three allies to maintain a united front against Germany. It is hard to explain the mentality of the German leadership: on the one hand, it could grasp that pressing on could well to lead to a pointless catastrophe, but, on the other hand, it did not have the will to admit this openly. Germany's hatred of England would simply not allow it.

The anti-British thrust of German policy cannot be overstressed. In fact, the central German war aim in 1914–18 was the destruction of England and its empire, hence the frenetic energy and wealth expended on building a high seas fleet. Leading politicians and intellectuals saw Germany on the cusp of a great turning point in history that would lead to the establishment of Germany's ambition to become a global, rather than a European, power. The world would at last be free of the deadening hand of British commerce and intellectual mediocrity, and in its place would be established the enriching and edifying German cultural heritage. Rivalry with Britain, then, no less than enmity with France, drove German war planning.

Wartime diplomacy

All these ideas gained concrete expression in official government policy almost immediately after the war broke out. In a document only discovered in the Berlin archives after 1945 called the 'September Program', the long-established aims of the German government were set out in detail. They were, in fact, the distillation of many memoranda already tabled in various ministries, and they foresaw the complete destruction of Russia and its empire in the east; similarly, the crushing of France and the occupation of large tracts of French territory in the east, so France could never again rise as an industrial power; the permanent occupation of Belgium, in particular for the purpose of establishing large naval bases on the English Channel from where to menace Britain. Holland, being a Germanic state with overseas territories, was to be bound to Germany in a special relationship. Specifically, the Dutch

East Indies – present-day Indonesia – was to be made available to the German navy to allow the construction of powerful naval bases with which to hold down Britain's Pacific Dominions as well as India. The colonies of France, Belgium, and Portugal in Africa were to be ceded to Berlin – the so-called *Mittel Afrika* concept – with the French colonies in the Asia Pacific region to follow suit.

It is important to remember that the *Mittel-Europa* grand design was actually implemented for a time after the defeat of Russia in 1918 in the famous treaty of Brest-Litovsk, courtesy of Trotsky, Lenin, and the Bolshevik Revolution. Germany occupied all the territories from the Baltic Seas to the Black Sea, stripping Russia of its western colonies such as Courland, Poland, and the Ukraine. On the throne of all these countries, a prince of the various houses of the Eastern German principalities was to be installed. This treaty is historically important because it gives us a concrete image of what the future of Europe would have looked like in the event of German war plans coming together.

Ludendorff's last gamble

The euphoria among the German power elite after Brest-Litovsk was ecstatic. They now only had to conquer the Allied forces in the west, and this explains the massive offensives from the spring of 1918, when enormous reinforcements taken from the east to deploy on the Western Front went into action – and almost succeeded. On 21 March 1918, after a relatively brief bombardment of five hours, as opposed to the usual five days, 1.6 million German soldiers attacked the Allied defences in five separate offences over a front for forty miles. And they did break through. In five days, some German units had pushed more than forty miles, with a successful complementary attack talking place in Flanders. German forces had driven the British and French back almost to the English Channel. The Allies were literally fighting with their backs to the wall. What happened next was predictable and predicted, as the Germans once again began to outrun their cover and supplies, and began, at each one of these five points of German offensive, to encounter stiff resistance. Knowing that this was probably Germany's last chance to win the war, General Eric von Ludendorff ordered a last desperate attack, in July, in the Second Battle of the Marne. It was repulsed. The French, British, and now the Americans, who entered the war in April 1917, counter-attacked, frustrating Ludendorff's plan for a great attack in Flanders, while enabling the newly appointed commander in chief of Allied armies in France, Ferdinand Foch, to take the initiative in the months ahead.

The Germans made one last, futile attempt to break the Allies' stand in France at the Battle of Amiens, where the Australians were used to make the crucial breakthrough at St Quentin, thus making 8 August the blackest day of the German army. From then on, the German armies were rolled back until finally their generals called for an armistice that was signed on 11 November 1918, at 11 a.m. The war could not be won, although the German navy had decided after the armistice to break out into the Channel to stop reinforcements coming from England, believing that the German army would be able to keep the territory it still occupied in Belgium and France. This move by the admirals, in turn, provoked the German revolution on 15 November. The troops had had enough and had finally refused to be sacrificed for the impossible dreams of the officer corps and the German power elite. So erupted the 'November Revolution', which caused the Kaiser and all the princes to abdicate. The outcome of the Revolution was that elections were called, after tedious negotiations of the various parties, and were held in January 1919. The new government under a republican constitution was compelled to sign the Treaty of Versailles on 28 June 1919, the fifth anniversary of that fateful day in Sarajevo.

A world safe for democracy

Principle was clearly lacking in the early years of World War I. The British were confused about why they were fighting Germany. In

1908, Prime Minister David Lloyd George expressed the predominant view of Britain towards Germany:

> Here is Germany in the middle of Europe, with France and Russia on either side, and with a combination of greater armies than hers.... Would we not be frightened, would we not build, would we not arm?

When London entered the war, it was, technically, in response to Germany's violation of Belgium's neutrality, though the original Treaty of London of 1839 left its signatories free to decide which course of action to pursue. Strictly speaking, then, Britain was under no obligation to go to war against Germany, though war was a legitimate option. Yet, even this was too slender to justify world war. Fully aware of this, Lloyd George attempted to expand the war aims to include independence for Poland and self-government for the nationalities of Austria-Hungary. Above all, this war must insure a just and lasting peace. But it was American President Woodrow Wilson who provided the lofty ideals and honourable goals that rallied the Allies to fight the war. In his war address to the United States Congress in April 1917, he detailed in clear terms a rationale for fighting:

> We are glad, now that we see the facts with no veil of false pretence about them, to fight for the ultimate peace of the world and for the liberation of peoples, the German peoples included: for the rights of nations great and small and the privilege of men everywhere to choose their way of life and of obedience. The world must be made safe for democracy. We have no selfish ends to serve. We desire no conquest, no dominion.... We are but one of the champions of the rights of mankind.

And there was more.

Wilson, with his acute sensitivity to the drift of history, saw a new era dawning – an era of responsibility, freedom, and, above all, peace. The League of Nations was to be the new tool for the new era. A partnership of democratic nations, it would be a league of honour, a partnership of opinion. Wilson was not aloof, however, to the sacrifices of war:

> It is a fearful thing to lead this great people into war, into the most terrible and disastrous of all war, civilization itself seeming to be in the balance. But the right is more precious than peace. . . .

The great departure in American diplomacy would have its price.

Fourteen Points

The war aims of the Allies were crowned by Wilson's 'Fourteen Points', which had been presented to Congress in January 1918. Among the issues stressed were open diplomacy, freedom of the seas, equality of trade conditions, reduction of armaments, adjustment of colonial claims, evacuation of Russia, Belgium, Alsace-Lorraine, Romania, and Serbia, and the establishment of an independent Polish state with access to the sea. The most important of the points was last, which specified that a general association of nations would be formed to insure the independence of nations. Wilson presented these principles as much to define the aims of the war as to define the terms of peace. While Germany, in agreeing to an armistice, accepted the Fourteen Points, the Allies did not. Britain rejected the principle of freedom of the seas, while France demanded reparations for damages. At the same time, Wilson suffered a blow in his support at home in November 1918 when Republicans scored victories in congressional elections across the nation.

Under fire at home and abroad, Wilson felt he had to compromise. For example, he allowed Italy to seize Austria-Tyrol (though he did block their claim to Fiume), he gave Silesia and the Polish Corridor to Poland, and allowed Japan to take German territories in Shantung. While he prevented France from permanently seizing the Rhine, he shut his eyes to secret treaties dividing the spoils of the German Empire. Wilson was apparently willing to sacrifice provisions of the Fourteen Points in order to ensure the formation of the League of Nations. Whatever the faults of the Treaty of Versailles, Wilson was confident that they would be rectified by the League. Ironically, it was his own government – the US Senate – that ultimately killed American participation in the League and, with it, Wilson's hope for a new era of lasting peace, based on universal principles in place of great power manoeuvring.

Lloyd George also bent to pressure from his own countrymen to punish Germany. Winston Churchill would later recall Lloyd George's situation:

> The Prime Minister and his principal colleagues were astonished and to some extent overborne by the passion they encountered in the constituencies. The brave people whom nothing had daunted had suffered too much. Their unspent feelings were lashed by the popular press into fury. The crippled and mutilated soldiers darkened the streets. The returned prisoners told the hard tales of bonds and privation. Every cottage had its empty chair. Hatred of the beaten foe, thirst for his just punishment, rushed up from the heart of deeply injured millions.

Nor was George as sympathetic to the Germans as Wilson. After all, Britain had suffered more than three million casualties (including nearly one million dead), while the United States suffered a little more than 300,000 casualties (including 115,000 dead). Defying Wilson's call for self-determination, Britain and the Dominions and France divided the German colonies among themselves after the war. Wilson could at most wrest a system of mandates, in which the colonial powers would deliver an annual account to the League.

Significantly, Lloyd George would not go as far as the French demanded. In a letter (referred to as the Fountainbleau

Memorandum) to the American and French leadership, though directed at the latter, George warned against creating new states containing large masses of German people, and opposed continuing payment of reparations beyond the war generation. 'Our terms may be severe', he observed,

> they may be stern, even ruthless, but at the same time they can be so just that the country on which they are imposed will feel in its heart it has no right to complain. But injustice, arrogance, displayed in the hour of triumph will never be forgotten or forgiven.

It is doubtful that it had much impact on French thinking.

French revenge

The French, represented by 'the tiger', Georges Clemenceau, were the most vindictive of the powers represented at the Paris Peace Conference. More than the United States, Great Britain, and Italy, France had been devastated by the war. France had suffered more than four million casualties, including 1,385,000 dead. And this was not the first time France had been attacked by Germany. The French were still smarting from the Franco-Prussian War (1870–1), in which the French were crushed. In the peace that followed, Germany, it was well remembered, demanded that France pay an enormous war indemnity (five billion gold francs) and relinquish its border territory, Alsace-Lorriane. Thus, following France's victory in World War I, Clemenceau naturally sought to cripple Germany militarily, politically, and economically, for vengeance and to prevent Germany from ever being a threat to France again.

In the end, it was the French who wielded the most influence on the Treaty of Versailles. France received back Alsace-Lorraine and acquired economic control of the coal-rich Saar territory, although the League would maintain political control of the formerly German region until a plebiscite was held in 1934.

France also took occupation for fifteen years of the German Rhineland, an industrial area along the French border. Three predominately Polish-German provinces were given to the newly reconstructed state of Poland. The Allies also took land from Russia, which had broken from the Allies and declared a separate peace, to form new states. For the most part, however, the treaty-makers were sensitive to the demands of ethnic groups in different areas for self-determination.

But the defeated Germans received no such considerations. The treaty detached the port of Danzig from Germany and made it a League 'free city', to give Poland access to the sea. It expressly forbade Austria – or what was left of it after the break-up of the Hapsburg Monarchy – to unite with Germany. It stripped the defeated nation of all its colonies. Germany was to have no heavy weapons, no air force, and no army over 100,000 men. Finally, and most controversially at the time – and significantly for the future – France and Britain levied on Germany reparations to cover the entire cost of the war, including such secondary expenses as pensions. Because the estimated sum was the incalculable, the Allies left the exact amount open; yet there was no question Germany would be severely taxed. For openers, Germany was to give the Allies its entire merchant marine, all private property owned by its nationals in foreign countries, and large payments in cash and gold.

War guilt

As justification for the huge reparations judgement – and in case anyone missed the point – the Allies included a punitive clause in the treaty. Article 231 reads:

> The Allied and Associated Governments affirm and Germany accepts the responsibility of Germany and her allies for causing all the loss and damage to which Allied and Associated Governments and their nationals have been subjected as a consequence of the war imposed on them by the aggression of Germany and her allies.

6. The Big Four at Versailles – Woodrow Wilson, Lloyd George, Georges Clemenceau, and Vittorio Orlando of Italy

This held that despite the various causes of the war, despite the German peoples' repudiation of the Kaiser and the establishment of parliamentary democracy, the German people alone were to be held responsible – solely responsible – for the most destructive war in history.

Even before the Treaty of Versailles was signed, there were objections to it in Britain by a small minority of dissenters. Government opposition parties – Labour and Independent – criticized the document as fiercely political. A number of Labourites, indeed, had ties with the German working class, and decried what they believed was basically a punitive treaty. More significant was the eloquent and stinging critique published in 1919 by economist John Maynard Keynes, a former Treasury official and representative to the Paris Peace Conference, who resigned in protest at the treaty's economic terms. In *The Economic Consequences of the Peace*, Keynes denounced the treaty and its creators. He was kindest with Lloyd George who, he said, had decided on moderation too late. Wilson, on the other hand, he described as a pathetic figure who was 'ill informed', as well as 'slow and unadaptable'. 'He had no plan', complained Keynes, 'no scheme, no constructive ideas whatever for clothing with the flesh of life the commandments which he had thundered from the White House'. The author reserved most of his scorn, however, for Clemenceau, the man who viewed the affairs of Europe as 'a perpetual prize fight, of which France had won this round, but of which this round is certainly not the last'. According to Keynes, the French leader sought more than revenge from a wartime enemy – he sought the virtual destruction of a political and economic rival: 'He sees the issue in terms of France and Germany, not of humanity and of European civilization struggling forwards to a new order.' For Keynes, then, nothing less than the future of Europe was at stake.

The brunt of Keynes's argument was especially directed towards the reparations clauses of the treaty. He took issue with the fact that no set amount was agreed upon. Never before, he said, had a carte blanche been part of a treaty:

> It is evident that Germany's pre-war capacity to pay an annual foreign tribute has not been unaffected by the almost total loss of her colonies, her overseas connections, her mercantile marine, and her foreign properties, by the cession of ten percent of her territory and population, of one-third of her coal and of three quarters of her iron ore, by two million casualties amongst men in the prime of life, by the starvation of her people for four years, by the burden of a vast war debt, by the depreciation of her currency to less than one-seventh of its former value, by the disruption of her allies and their territories, by Revolution at home and Bolshevism on her borders, and by all the unmeasured ruin in strength and of four years hope of all-swallowing war and final defeat.

7. John Maynard Keynes

Yet, continued Keynes, most estimates of a great indemnity from Germany rested on the false assumption that it would be in a position to conduct in the future a vastly greater trade than it ever had in the past.

Keynes was also concerned that never before had Britain levied such widely defined reparations. According to the treaty, the Reparations Commission was empowered to obtain $5 billion from Germany in any form (cash, property, raw materials) by May 1921. 'This provision', protested Keynes, 'has the effect of entrusting to the Reparations Commission for the period in question dictatorial powers over all German property of every description whatever'. But this appeared to be only the first payment of an enormous and unrealistic bill to the Allies. The former Treasury official also predicted a period of deep economic depression for Germany as a consequence of the treaty; millions would be unemployed and many would die as the Weimar Republic's economy was strangled by Allied plans for peace. Indeed, it seemed to Keynes that the peace-makers had deliberately set out to destroy Germany: 'The economic clauses of the treaty are comprehensive, and little has been overlooked which might impoverish Germany now or obstruct her development in the future.' Finally, Keynes called attention to the fact that Germany's fate was intertwined with Europe's; with Germany crippled, the entire European economy would suffer. His official outlook was grim: 'An inefficient, unemployed, disorganized Europe faces us, torn by internal strife, and international hate, fighting, starving, pillaging, and lying.'

A mistake

Though his argument was exaggerated and later subject to revision, Keynes changed the drift of British opinion. His book ultimately destroyed British faith in the treaty, and the righteousness of the war itself, and unleashed a torrent of opposition to the peace terms. Where once they had felt the exultation and vengeance of victory, the British developed fear and guilt over what they had wrought. The British feared that the treaty's terms might cause themselves economic hardship. Moreover, London was now concerned with a new enemy, potentially more dangerous than Germany: the Soviet Union. Enforcement of the treaty, the British worried, might even drive Germany into the arms of the Bolsheviks. In addition, many Englishmen had moral qualms about the treaty. Keynes had given them misgivings about taking territory from Germany, while demanding reparations for the cost of the war. Was it right to impose such hardships on a country already devastated by war? The British had traditionally been more forgiving. The intensity of French vindictiveness made many sympathetic towards the Germans. Of course, the Germans sought to exploit these emotions by launching a massive propaganda campaign in Great Britain. While it did have an effect, it only heightened the already strong doubts about the morality of the terms of peace. Within a generation, even many in France came to the same conclusion.

Beyond the specific provisions of the treaty, the underlying principle of the peace – that Germany was solely responsible for the outbreak of the war – increasingly disturbed the British. Many were of the opinion that neither Germany nor any other nation caused the war, but that it was a spontaneous action by all those involved. Fourteen years after he had negotiated the terms of the Treaty of Versailles, David Lloyd George argued that World War I was a mistake:

> I am convinced after a careful perusal of all the documents available on all sides that the Kaiser never had the remotest idea he was plunging – or being plunged – into a European war.... He was not anticipating a costly war but a cheap diplomatic triumph.

In the end, the negotiations were botched by everybody engaged in directing them. For the former Prime Minister: 'War ought to have been, and could have been averted.' By 1937, few in Europe and even America would have disagreed.

Chapter 4

The night Stalin and Churchill divided Europe

Of the many fascinating episodes that punctuate the diplomacy of World War II, few have intrigued scholars more than the secret Balkan spheres-of-action agreement worked out by Prime Minister Winston Churchill and Marshal Josef Stalin at the Anglo-Soviet conference (British code-named TOLSTOY) held in Moscow in the autumn of 1944. It was late in the evening of 9 October. In his first encounter with Stalin since the meeting of the Big Three at Teheran in 1943, Churchill, believing 'the moment . . . apt for business', appealed to the Soviet dictator in the simple language of power politics: 'Let us settle about our affairs in the Balkans.' Specifically, he went on:

> We have interests, missions, and agents there. Don't let us get at cross-purposes in small ways. So far as Britain and Russia are concerned, how would it do for you to have ninety per cent dominance in Rumania, for us to have ninety per cent of the say in Greece, and go fifty-fifty about Yugoslavia?

In the time this was being translated, the British leader recalled in his memoirs:

> I wrote on a half-sheet of paper—
> Rumania

Russia 90%
The others 10%
    Greece

Great Britain (in accord with USA) 90%
Russia 10%

    Yugoslavia 50–50%
    Hungary 50–50%
    Bulgaria

Russia 75%
The others 25%

In the presence of the small gathering that had come together that night in the Kremlin, Stalin looked on, listening for the translation. Having finally understood, he paused slightly and 'took his blue pencil and made a large tick upon it, and passed it back to us'. Thus, concluded Churchill, 'It was all settled in no more time than it takes to set down'. With only minor variations – 80%–20% predominance in favour of the Soviets in Hungary and Bulgaria, reached by Foreign Secretary Anthony Eden and Minister for Foreign Affairs Vyacheslav Molotov, in two additional meetings amidst resolution of the tangled Bulgarian armistice dispute – the original agreement remained intact, or so it was thought.

Upon his return to London, the Prime Minister reported confidently to the House of Commons that, so far as the Balkans was concerned, he and Stalin had been able to reach complete agreement. Moreover, he added,

> I do not feel there is any immediate danger of our combined war effort being weakened by divergence of policy or of doctrine in Greece, Rumania, Bulgaria, Yugoslavia and, beyond the Balkans, Hungary. We have reached a very good working arrangement about all these countries, singly and in combination, with the object of concentrating all their efforts, and concerting them with ours

8. The Big Three at Teheran in 1943 – Churchill, Stalin, and Franklin D. Roosevelt

against the common foe, and providing, as far as possible, for a peaceful settlement.

Though it is commonly agreed that the subject of Balkan percentages was not again officially raised at Yalta, in February 1945 – or at any other time during the remainder of World War II – historians continue to debate the significance of the personal diplomacy concluded at TOLSTOY, the most important of the wartime conferences.

Churchill's 'need of another personal meeting with Stalin'

What prompted Churchill to travel to Moscow in October 1944 in search of a Balkan agreement? Few scholars have had any reason to doubt the Prime Minister's own account of his decision to embark on this journey. Against the background of the aftermath of the Soviet offensive of the summer of 1944, which witnessed the occupation of Bucharest and a declaration of war against Bulgaria, to be followed shortly by an armistice, Churchill 'felt the need of another personal meeting with Stalin, whom I had not seen since Teheran [in 1943], and with whom, in spite of the Warsaw tragedy, I felt new links since the successful opening of "Overlord"'.

The Prime Minister observed furthermore that while, 'the arrangements which I had made with the President in the summer to divide our [Anglo-Soviet] responsibilities for looking after particular countries [Greece and Rumania, respectively] affected by the movements of the armies had tided us over the three months for which our arrangement ran', the time had come to rethink the agreement anew. The first Balkan agreement, so called, originated with the British leader's concern in early May that something had to be done to put the Russians in their place. 'I am not very clear on it myself', the Prime Minister minuted Eden on 4 May, 'but evidently we are approaching a showdown with the Russians about their Communist intrigue in Italy, Yugoslavia and Greece. . . . I must say their attitude becomes more difficult every day.' Initially, Churchill requested that the Foreign Minister draft a paper 'for the Cabinet and possibly for the Imperial Conference setting forth shortly, . . . the brute issues between us and the Soviet Government which are developing in Italy, in Rumania, in Bulgaria, in Yugoslavia and above all in Greece'.

For Churchill, the issue was unequivocal: 'Are we going to acquiesce in the Communization of the Balkans and perhaps of Italy?' The paper, which was placed before the War Cabinet on 7 June, suggested that an effort ought to be made, 'to focus our [British] influence in the Balkans by consolidating our position in Greece and Turkey . . . and, while avoiding any direct challenge to Russian influence in Yugoslavia, Albania, Rumania and Bulgaria, to avail ourselves of every opportunity in order to spread British influence in those countries.' Even while the paper was being drafted, Eden sought out the Soviet Ambassador in London in order to establish the Balkan ground rules.

On 5 May, only a day after Churchill had minuted his concern, Eden called on Soviet Ambassador Gousev and raised,

> the possibility of our agreeing between ourselves as a practical matter that Rumanian affairs would be in the main the concern of the Soviet Government, while Greek affairs would be in the main our concern, each Government giving the other help in the respective countries.

Less than two weeks later, the Soviets replied to the suggestion positively with the proviso, to quote Eden's cable to his ambassador in Moscow, that,

> before giving any final assurance in the matter, they would like to know whether we had consulted the United States Government and whether the latter also agreed to this arrangement. If so, the Soviet Government would be ready to give us a final affirmative answer.

The Foreign Secretary's final remarks are instructive:

> I [Eden] said that I did not think we had consulted the United States Government in the matter but would certainly be ready to do so. *I could not imagine that they would dissent.* After all, the matter was really related to the military operations of our respective forces. Rumania fell within the sphere of the Russian armies and Greece within the Allied Command under General Wilson in the Mediterranean. Therefore it seemed natural that Soviet Russia should take the lead in Rumania and we in Greece, and that each should support the other.

In as much as it was common knowledge that the old Wilsonian Secretary of State Cordell Hull was, in fact, flatly opposed to any division of Europe or section of Europe into spheres of influence – or, to paraphrase his comments to Congress upon his return from the Foreign Ministers' conference at Moscow in late 1943, 'any other of the special arrangements through which, in the unhappy past, the nations strove to safeguard their security or to promote their interests' – it is in itself hard to imagine how Eden ever expected to carry the Americans along. It is also tempting to think that the Kremlin had deliberately nudged the Foreign Secretary into a trap.

In any case, the British Ambassador Lord Halifax called on Hull on 30 May to broach the subject. Concealing the fact that Eden had already spoken to the Russians, and representing the suggestions as the fruit of the Foreign Secretary's 'own independent reflection', Halifax inquired how the United States 'would feel about an arrangement between the British and the Russians to the effect that Russia might have a controlling influence in Rumania and Great Britain a controlling influence in Greece'. Though promising to give the matter serious attention, Hull voiced deep reservations about the wisdom of abandoning 'the fixed rules and policies which are in accord with our broad basic declarations of policy, principles and practice'. Before receiving Halifax's report of his meeting with Hull, and still anticipating no difficulty in State, Eden requested the Prime Minister to send a personal message to Roosevelt in order to 'reinforce' the Foreign Office's representations to Hull. It was at this juncture, however, that Churchill and Eden crossed signals, raising serious doubts, at least in some American minds, as to the true aims of British policy in the Balkans.

Secret revealed

After observing that there had 'recently been disquieting signs between ourselves and the Russians in regard to the Balkan countries and in particular Greece', Churchill let the proverbial cat out of the bag when he told FDR that:

[W]e therefore suggested to the Soviet Ambassador here that we should agree between ourselves as a practical matter that the Soviet Government would take the lead in Rumanian affairs, while we would take the lead in Greek affairs, each Government giving the other help in the respective countries.

In asking Roosevelt to give this proposal his 'blessing', the Prime Minister took pains to point out to the election-bound President that:

We do not of course wish to carve up the Balkans into spheres of influence and in agreeing to the arrangement we should make it clear that it applied only to war conditions and did not affect the rights and responsibilities which each of the three Great Powers will have to exercise at the peace settlement and afterwards in regard to the whole of Europe.

The thrust of this was repeated to Halifax a week later. In the meantime, Halifax conveyed to Eden his only reason for concealing Whitehall's initiative in approaching the Soviets first: 'I purposely did not disclose the fact that you had already taken the matter up with the Russians', he cabled Eden on 5 June, 'because, I thought, we were more likely to get the Americans along with us in that way'. Furthermore, he went on to remonstrate:

Subject to what you and the Prime Minister may feel and to obvious necessities of urgency that may arise, it would seem wise, when you have instructed me to take up something with Mr Hull, to defer action through the higher channel of the President until I have been able to report progress with Mr Hull, and further action that you may wish to take can be taken with the knowledge of what has passed at lower level. Otherwise we risk confusion and embarrassment.

Halifax got both for his trouble.

After some debate in State between the European and Near Eastern Desks, Acting Secretary of State Edward Stettinius handed the file over to Assistant Secretary of State Breckenridge Long for a recommendation. During the next several days, Long prepared an answer in the negative, which in turn was approved without change by the President on 10 June. Roosevelt advised Churchill in no uncertain language that his government was 'unwilling to approve the proposed arrangement'. Washington's position was as follows:

> Briefly, we acknowledge that the militarily responsible Government in any given territory will inevitably make decisions required by military developments but are convinced that the natural tendency for such decisions to extend to other than military field would be strengthened by an agreement of the type suggested. On our opinion, this would certainly result in the persistence of differences between you and the Soviets and, in the division of the Balkans into spheres of influence despite the declared intention to limit the arrangements to military matters.

What to offer in its place? 'We believe', the President gently lectured the Prime Minister, 'efforts should preferably be made to establish consultative machinery to dispel misunderstandings and restrain the tendency toward the development of exclusive spheres'. Though, to be sure, without any risk of disturbing his special relationship with Roosevelt, Churchill replied with a forcefulness of his own.

'Action is paralysed', he cabled the same day, 'if everybody is to consult everybody else about everything before it is taken. The events will always outstrip the changing situation in these Balkan regions'. Besides which, 'Somebody must have the power to plan and act'; consultative machinery 'would be a mere obstruction, always overridden in any case of emergency by direct interchange between you and me, or either you and Stalin'. Explaining the realities of the prospect of Soviet troops on

Romanian soil – 'they will probably do what they like anyhow' – and the British investment both of blood and treasure in Greece, Churchill appealed to the President's vanity with several questions: 'Why is all this effective direction to be broken up into a committee of mediocre officials such as we are littering about the world? Why can you and I not keep this in our hands considering how we see eye to eye about so much of it?'

In conclusion, the Prime Minister proposed that the President agree to a trial period of three months, although clearly, it seems, Churchill would have settled for two months as preferable to nothing. Roosevelt was apparently impressed with the Prime Minister's logic. For, without notifying State for over two weeks that he had reversed course, the President acquiesced in Churchill's proposal, with the provision, '[W]e must be careful to make it clear that we are not establishing any postwar spheres of influence'. Needless to say, Churchill, who doubtless must have congratulated himself both on his power of persuasion and his ability to override the State Department, was grateful. All that remained was to pass on the information to the Soviets.

'The United States Government have now been consulted', Eden wrote to the Soviet Ambassador in London on 19 June, 'and they agree with the arrangement proposed'. More to the point, the Secretary noted, 'They feel some anxiety, however, lest it should extend beyond the immediate circumstances for which it has been devised and should lead to the partition of the Balkan countries into spheres of influence', a prospect at variance with London's intentions 'that the arrangement should apply only to war conditions and should not affect the rights and responsibilities which each of our three Governments will have to exercise at the peace settlement and afterwards in regard to the whole of Europe'. In any case, he finished in a manner intimating only a hint of disagreement:

In order to guard against any danger of the arrangement extending beyond the purpose for which it has been devised we have suggested to the United States Government, and they have agreed, that it should be given a trial of three months after which it would be reviewed by our three Governments. I hope, therefore, that the Soviet Government will agree to the arrangement coming into force on this basis.

The Soviet Government had other plans, however. Ambassador Gousev replied on 8 July that in light of changed circumstances, particularly certain apprehensions expressed by the United States, the Kremlin would consider it necessary to give the question further consideration. Moreover, he added, 'the Soviet Government deem it advisable to make a direct approach to the United States Government in order to obtain more detailed information as to their attitude to this question'. This was done on 1 July. Moscow had called Eden's bluff.

The State Department, with Hull back in the picture and the President in the midst of an election campaign, replied to the Soviet request two weeks later, on 15 July, observing that 'It is correct that the Government of the United States assented to the [Balkan] arrangement, for a trial period of three months, this assent being given in consideration of present war strategy.' This particular 'overriding consideration' aside, State continued, the United States

> would wish to make known its apprehension lest the proposed agreement might, by the natural tendency of such arrangements, lead to the division, in fact, of [the] Balkan region into spheres of influence, [which] would be an unfortunate development, in view of decisions of Moscow Conference . . .

As a consequence of those decisions, State had hoped that no projected measure would

> be allowed to prejudice efforts towards direction of policies of the Allied governments along lines of collaboration rather than

independent action, since any arrangement suggestive of spheres of influence cannot but militate against establishment and effective functioning of a broader system of general security in which all countries will have their part.

Still – no doubt with due respect to the President's previous determination to do otherwise – the Secretary of State let it be known that he would have no particular objection to a three months' trial period so long as Anglo-Soviet actions in no way affected 'the rights and responsibilities which each of the three principal allies will have to exercise during the period of re-establishment of peace and afterwards in regard to the whole of Europe'. And, finally, in case anyone missed the point, State went on notice in assuming aloud 'that the arrangement would have neither direct or indirect validity as affecting interests of this Government or of other Governments associated with the three principal allies'. In addition to the arguments against spheres of influence contained in this memorandum, there were other, perhaps less lofty, considerations to be taken into account.

In a top-secret letter written to Hull in May 1944, Admiral William D. Leahy, Roosevelt's chief of staff, advanced a number of military arguments in opposition to spheres of influence along the lines of the proposed Anglo-Soviet agreement. According to Leahy, whose diary records that he did 'not intend to sacrifice American soldiers and sailors in order to impose any government on any people, or to adjust political differences in Europe or Asia, except to act against an aggressor with the purpose of preventing an international war', the nation's best interests in postwar would be served by maintaining 'the solidarity of [the] three great powers', until such time as 'arrangements will be perfected for the prevention of world conflicts'. Furthermore, and as any world conflict in the foreseeable future would most likely find Britain and Soviet Russia in opposite camps, with Moscow in an overwhelmingly dominant military position on the continent, about which the United States could presently do little, it would be prudent for America to 'exert its utmost efforts and utilize all its influence to prevent such a situation arising and to promote a spirit of mutual cooperation between Britain, Russia and ourselves'.

Put another way, Leahy was saying that in the case of war between London and Moscow, probably occasioned by a territorial dispute on the continent,

> we might be able to successfully defend Britain [proper], but we could not, under existing conditions, defeat Russia. . . . we would find ourselves [therefore] engaged in a war which we could not win even though the United States would be in no danger of defeat and occupation.

To attempt to eschew such a situation was simply to recognize one of the new international facts of life:

> the recent phenomenal development of the heretofore latent Russian military and economic strength – a development which seems certain to prove epochal in its bearing on future politico-military international relationships, and which has yet to reach the full scope with Russian resources.

While it is doubtful that Leahy's remarks represented a significant reversal of the nation's official attitude towards balance-of-power politics, they are significant in the sense that they indicate an official awareness of the limits of American power to influence events in postwar continental Europe, including the Balkans.

FDR's disapproval

Meanwhile, President Roosevelt expressed his strong disapproval of the manner in which the British had handled the proposed Balkan arrangement. 'I think I should tell you frankly', FDR cabled Churchill on 22 June, 'that we were disturbed that your people took this matter up with us only after it had been put up to the Russians and they had inquired [at this late juncture] whether we were agreeable'. More or less accepting the Foreign Office's explanation 'that the proposal "arose out of a chance remark" which was converted by the Soviet Government into a formal proposal', the President hoped that 'matters of this importance can be prevented from developing in such a manner in the future'. The Prime Minister was quick to reply, pointing out in addition to the long-belaboured observations that the Soviets were the only power that could do anything in Romania and that the Greek burden rested almost entirely on the British, that he had had no complaints of Roosevelt's recent private messages to Stalin with regard to the Poles. 'I am not complaining at all of this', he assured the President, 'because I know we are working for the general theme and purposes and I hope you will feel that this has been so in my conduct of the Greek affair'.

Appealing to FDR's political instincts, the Prime Minister conceded that, 'It would be quite easy for me, on the general principle of slithering to Left, which is so popular in foreign policy, to let things rip when the King of Greece would probably be forced to abdicate' and the Communist-led elements 'would work a reign of terror'; accordingly, the only way to prevent such a state of affairs was to persuade Moscow to quit boosting the Communists 'and ramming it forward with all their force'. It was in these circumstances, he concluded, 'I proposed to the Russians a temporary working arrangement for the better conduct of the war. This was only a proposal and had to be referred to you for agreement.' Roosevelt seems to have grasped the message when several days later he replied to the Prime Minister, saying, 'It appears that both of us have inadvertently taken unilateral action in a direction that we both now agree to have been expedient for the time being.' Nonetheless, he made clear, 'It is essential that we should always be in agreement in matters bearing on our allied war matters.' The incident seemed closed.

Several weeks later, upon receipt of news from Eden that the Kremlin had now found it necessary to give the question of a Balkan division 'further consideration' and was, in fact, approaching the United States direct, Churchill virtually went through the ceiling. 'Does this mean', he minuted the Foreign Secretary on 9 July:

> that all we had settled with the Russians now goes down through the pedantic interference of the United States, and that Rumania and Greece are to be condemned to a regime of triangular telegrams in which the United States and ourselves are to interfere with the Russian treatment of Rumania, and the Russians are to boost up E.A.M. [the National Liberation Front] while the President pursues a pro-King policy in regard to Greece, and we have to make all things go sweet? If so, it will be a great disaster.

The following day, 10 July, Eden informed the War Cabinet that the proposed Anglo-Soviet spheres-of-action agreement with regard to Greece and Romania had, in the Foreign Secretary's words, 'broken down'.

Puzzled by the actual meaning of State's response to the Soviet inquiry of 1 July – 'Does this mean that the Americans have agreed to the three months' trial, or is it all thrown in the pool again?'– and increasingly concerned by the prospect of Soviet interference in Greek affairs, particularly the unheralded dispatch of a mission of Russian officers there in late July, Churchill would have to await the changing tides of war before making another approach to the USSR on a Balkan settlement. Moreover, in the light of past experience with the Americans, it is hardly surprising that the next time the Prime Minister sought to play his hand in the Balkans, he would approach Stalin himself, a man with whom Churchill 'considered one could talk as one human being to another'. Until such time, and for all intents and purposes, the May Agreement had all but become a dead letter.

By October 1944, the Prime Minister's time had come. For better and for worse, the war situation had fundamentally been altered since spring. With respect to the latter, the Red Army had firmly established itself in Romania and Bulgaria and had only recently penetrated Yugoslavia and Hungary; by the same token, British influence in the region had been confined to Greece and Yugoslavia, principally in the form of military liaison missions with the guerrilla organizations of those countries and, to a lesser extent, by hosting the Greek and Yugoslav governments in exile. Of particular urgency to Churchill was the threat to Greece posed by the possible Bulgarian retention of parts or all of Macedonia and Thrace occupied during the course of the war. The fact that Bulgaria now marched on the side of the Allies proved cold comfort indeed, considering the Soviets were calling the tune.

All of this is not to say, however, that Churchill would be travelling to Moscow without some bargaining power of his own. For, if the Russians had made great advances in south-eastern Europe, the Western Powers had also won remarkable victories. Since May, the Second Front had been established, Paris and Brussels had both been liberated, and the frontier of the Reich breached. In fact, it began to appear that it might well be the Western half of the Grand Alliance that would reach Berlin first before the advancing Red Army. Furthermore, the Prime Minister could well boast that, at least until July 1944, the British Empire had more men in contact with the enemy the world over than had the United States. Add to this Churchill's natural tendency, as he cabled Stalin on 4 October, to return to Moscow under the much happier conditions created since August 1942, at which time, it was the Prime Minister's sober mission to apprise the great Soviet leader that there would be no Second Front in 1942. The great remaining question facing Churchill was, to paraphrase Halifax's words of the previous June, how 'to get the Americans along with us'. Predictably enough, the Prime Minister went straight to the President, with whom he had just experienced the most cordial relations at the Second Quebec Conference (11–19 September) and at Hyde Park, American resistance to eleventh-hour Balkan military operations to the contrary notwithstanding.

On 29 September, Churchill advised FDR that he and Eden were considering flying to Moscow, the two great objects of the exercise being, 'first, to clinch his [Stalin's] coming in against Japan and, secondly, to try to effect a friendly settlement with Poland. There are other points too about Greece and Yugoslavia which we could also discuss'. And lest there be any misunderstanding, the Prime Minister reassured the President, '[W]e should keep you informed of every point'. Churchill followed up several days later, requesting Roosevelt to send Stalin a message, saying that he had approved of the mission, and that the US Ambassador in Moscow would be available to take part in the proceedings. The Prime Minister again wanted the President's blessing, and almost got it.

In a draft reply prepared by Admiral Leahy, and approved without change by the White House, Roosevelt 'merely wished Churchill "good luck", saying he understood perfectly why the trip had to be made'. At this point, according to Robert Sherwood, presidential adviser Harry Hopkins, having 'learned that Roosevelt was dispatching a cable to Churchill in which he ... in effect wash[ed] his hands of the whole matter [Balkans], with the implication that he was content to let Churchill speak for the United States as well as for Great Britain', intercepted the message and directed that it not be sent, albeit a decision made after Hopkins had phoned FDR. Sensitive both to Ambassador Averell Harriman's September warnings from Moscow that the time had come to make clear to the Soviets 'what we expect of them as the price of our good will' and to Churchill's well-known inclination to make a Balkan deal, Hopkins persuaded Roosevelt it would be a mistake to send vague messages to Churchill and Stalin which would probably have the opposite effect of detaching the administration from the results of their meeting – whether on the Polish, Balkan, or any other controversial issue. With the elections a month away, and having just burned his fingers with the so-called Morgenthau Plan, to punish Germany severely, the President agreed to send Churchill and Stalin a different kind of message.

'I can well understand the reasons why you feel that an immediate meeting between yourself and Uncle Joe [Stalin] is necessary before the three of us can get together', FDR responded to Churchill on 4 October. 'The questions which you will discuss there', he continued, 'are ones which are, of course, of real interest to the United States, as I know you will agree. I have therefore instructed Harriman to stand by and to participate as my observer, if agreeable to you and Uncle Joe, and I have so informed Stalin'. Finally, the President concluded unequivocally, 'While naturally Averell [Harriman] will not be in a position to commit the United States – I could not permit any one to commit me in advance – he will be able to keep me fully informed and I have told him to return to me as soon as the conference is over.' All in all, the meeting in Moscow should prove 'a useful prelude' to another meeting with the Big Three after the elections. Churchill replied the next day, thanking Roosevelt for his thoughts on the matter and for his good wishes.

In as much as it was now apparent that he would not be receiving Roosevelt's blessing in advance, the Prime Minister then sought to protect his own freedom of manoeuvre: 'I am very glad that Averell [Harriman] should sit in at all principal conferences; but you will not I am sure, wish this to preclude private tête-à-têtes between me and UJ [Stalin] or Anthony [Eden] and Molotov, as it is often under such conditions that the best progress is made', though he went on to reassure the President once again that 'you can rely on me to keep you constantly informed of everything that affects our joint interests apart from the reports Averell will send'.

Roosevelt's message to Stalin, who seemed puzzled by it all, having supposed Churchill was coming in accordance with agreements reached at Quebec, expressed similar sentiments with regard to the Prime Minister's wishes to have an early conference and similar instructions with regard to allowing Ambassador Harriman to stand in as his observer. Perhaps preoccupied more with preserving his options in future than he ought to have been, the President underscored his personal concern with the coming talks. 'You, naturally, understand', he observed,

> that in this global war there is literally no question, political or military, in which the United States is not interested. I am firmly convinced that the three of us, and only the three of us, can find the solution to the still unresolved questions. In this sense, while appreciating the Prime Minister's desire for the meeting, I prefer to regard your forthcoming talks with Churchill as preliminary to a meeting of the three of us, which so far as I am concerned, can take place any time after the elections here.

Again, the British had failed to carry the Americans along in advance, but this time there would be absolutely no doubt, both in Moscow and London, where the United States stood.

Interestingly, the very diplomat who had assisted in the drafting of these messages to Stalin and Churchill, Charles E. Bohlen, Chief of the Division of Eastern European Affairs, was simultaneously pressing for an unequivocal statement of the administration's position in the Balkans, in the absence of which Washington would only have itself to blame for any subsequent misunderstanding. 'This Government', he contended in State, '[was] to some extent at fault because neither of our principal allies had yet a clear picture as to what the US will do and how much responsibility it will assume in Eastern Europe'. Furthermore, Bohlen indicated that in as much as the Soviets tended to be more inclined to 'accept comprehensive plans presented to them by others' rather than draw up their own, perhaps the time had come to raise 'the question as to whether we might not present to the Russians a plan for dealing with this area'. By this time, however, Churchill was already in Moscow presenting a plan of his own.

Stalin 'ready to discuss anything'

At the outset of his meeting with Stalin on the evening of 9 October, Churchill had 'hoped they might clear away many questions about which they had been writing to each other for a long time', to which Stalin replied 'that he was ready to discuss anything'. Turning from a discussion of the Polish Question, whose ramifications would ultimately dominate the conference proceedings until the departure of the British delegation on 18 October, Churchill declared, 'Britain must be the leading Mediterranean Power and . . . hoped Marshal Stalin would let him have first say about Greece in the same way as Marshal Stalin [would have the first say] about Rumania'. Without once alluding to the May Agreement, Stalin concurred, pointing out that 'if Britain were interested in the Mediterranean then Russia was equally interested in the Black Sea'. It was further agreed that the two powers should share equal interests in Hungary and Yugoslavia.

The sticking point, however, was Bulgaria, which posed the single greatest threat to the British position in Greece. According to the records of the meeting, 'The Prime Minister suggested that where Bulgaria was concerned the British interest was greater than it was in Rumania', where London's influence on the Soviet-controlled Allied Control Commission was admittedly nominal. Stalin, who suggested that the Prime Minister claimed too much for Britain in the area, countered that Bulgaria was after all a Black Sea country and, by extension, a matter of Russian concern. In response to Stalin's query, 'Was Britain afraid of anything?', Eden, who until now had remained silent, retorted 'that Britain was not afraid of anything'. He also reminded the Soviet leader 'that Britain had been at war with Bulgaria for three years [in contrast to recent Soviet–Bulgarian belligerency] and wanted a small share of the control of that country'. The Bulgarian armistice issue, together with a change in the ratio of Soviet predominance in Hungary

(80%–20%), was eventually settled by Eden and Molotov in the course of discussion over the next two days. Thus, a bargain of sorts had been struck over a division of Anglo-Soviet responsibilities in the Balkans; what it meant, exactly, was of course another matter.

From another level of analysis, it is interesting to note the missing President's influence on the participants' manoeuvrings. When it came to phrasing the division of responsibilities, Churchill, with the recent American experience fresh in his mind, thought it 'better to express these things in diplomatic [more euphemistic] terms and not to use the phrase "dividing into spheres", because the Americans might be shocked'. Still, 'as long as he and the Marshal understood each other he could explain matters to the President', no doubt at a time and place of the Prime Minister's choosing.

At this juncture, Stalin interrupted his guest 'to say that he [too] had received a message from President Roosevelt', indicating FDR's desire both to have the American Ambassador stand in as his observer and to regard the talks themselves as of a preliminary nature. Lest Stalin arrive at a false impression, Churchill advised the Soviet leader that he of course agreed with the President's wishes, observing that he and the President had no secrets. Nonetheless, he did not think Harriman, whose presence would be welcomed at a 'good number of their talks', should be allowed to come between them in their private talks – presumably such as the one in progress. Stalin confessed he did not like Roosevelt's message, as 'it seemed to demand too many rights for the United States leaving too little for the Soviet Union and Great Britain who, after all, had a treaty of common assistance'. Actually, as Stalin must have surely known, the President's message demanded nothing of the kind; if anything, and once the President's electoral sensitivity had been factored out, the message comes closer to John Lukac's image of America's 'supreme unconcern' in the region.

Towards the end of their conversation, the Prime Minister made two final points that were undoubtedly for the Marshal's consumption. First, and in connection with the proposed Allied occupation of Germany, he considered it unlikely that the Americans would stay in Germany, and by extension Europe, for 'very long', the implication being that European problems would have to be settled between themselves. Second, and with no thought of subtlety this time, Churchill personally wanted Stalin to know, to quote from the concluding comments in the record 'that the British had as many divisions fighting against Germany in Italy and France as the United States and we had nearly as many as the United States fighting against Japan'. Apparently, Churchill was anxious to assure his host that British credentials to speak for the solution of European problems were at least as good as the Americans, who, in any case, were not expected to remain.

What was accomplished?

What precisely, then, did the Prime Minister hope to accomplish by the percentage agreement, such as it was? Unfortunately, and although the documentary record suggests numerous clues, there is no definitive answer to this question. In an official joint communiqué to Roosevelt of their first meeting, Churchill, together with Stalin, merely informed the President: 'We have to consider the best way of reaching an agreed policy about the Balkan countries including Hungary and Turkey', apparently omitting the concluding phrase, 'having regard to our varying duty towards them', as reported by Harriman. But was there in fact 'an agreed policy'? In an unsent letter to Stalin dated 11 October, the British leader perhaps came nearer the truth when he noted that, 'The percentages which I have put down are no more than a method by which in our thoughts we can see how near we are together, and then decide upon the necessary steps to bring us into full agreement'; and though 'they could not be the basis of any public document, certainly not at the present time, they might however be a good guide for the conduct of our affairs'.

A day later, 12 October, the Prime Minister wrote to colleagues in London further elaborating his thoughts on the percentages. 'The system of percentages', he expanded,

> is not intended to prescribe the number sitting on [the Allied Control] Commissions for the different Balkan countries, but rather to express the interest and sentiment with which the British and Soviet Governments approach the problems of these countries and so that they might reveal their minds to each other in some way that could be comprehended.

More significantly, Churchill added:

> It is not intended to be more than a guide, and of course in no way commits the United States, nor does it set up a rigid system of spheres of interest. It may however help the United States to see how their two principal Allies feel about these regions when the picture is presented as a whole.

To this picture, echoed Eden to the British Under-Secretary of State, Sir Orme Sargent:

> Too much attention should not be paid to percentages which are of symbolic character only and bear no exact relation to number of persons of British and Soviet nationality to be employed [in the Control Commissions].

To the Americans, who were at this stage fairly much in the dark, Churchill projected an altogether different, but confident, image of the Balkan talks.

'Everything is most friendly here', the Prime Minister cabled Harry Hopkins on 11 October, 'but the Balkans are in a sad tangle'. In fact, he went on in a manner to justify the continual exclusion of the American Ambassador from the Balkan proceedings thus far, 'We have so many bones to pick about the Balkans at the present time that we would rather carry matters a little further a deux in order to be able to talk more bluntly than at a larger gathering.' On the same day, the Prime Minister indicated to the President that:

> It is absolutely necessary we should try to get a common mind about the Balkans, so that we may prevent civil war breaking out in several countries when probably you and I would be in sympathy with one side and U.J. [Stalin] with the other. I shall keep you informed of all this, and nothing will be settled except preliminary agreements between Britain and Russia, subject to further discussion and melting-down with you. On this basis I am sure you will not mind our trying to have a full meeting of minds with the Russians.

A week later, on the eve of his departure from Moscow, and still in no mood to offer more information than was absolutely necessary, the British leader apprised FDR that 'arrangements made about the Balkans are, I am sure, the best that are possible'. Specifically, the Prime Minister continued:

> Coupled with our successful military action recently we should now be able to save Greece and, I have no doubt, that agreement to pursue a fifty-fifty joint policy in Yugoslavia will be the best solution for our difficulties in view of Tito's behavior and changes in the local situation, resulting from the arrival of Russian and Bulgarian forces under Russian command to help Tito's eastern flank. The Russians are insistent on their ascendancy in Rumania and Bulgaria as the Black Sea countries.

Characteristically, the Soviets had even less to say.

'During the stay of Mr Churchill and Mr Eden in Moscow', Stalin cabled President Roosevelt on 19 October, 'we have exchanged views on a number of questions of mutual interest'. Doubtless aware that both Ambassador Harriman and the Prime Minister had already passed on their estimates of the most important Moscow conversations, the Soviet leader sought to impart his own.

'On my part', he observed with some economy of expression, 'I can say that our conversations were extremely useful in the mutual ascertaining of views on such questions as the attitude towards . . . policy in regard to the Balkan states', among other things. Furthermore, Stalin stated:

> During the conversations it has been clarified that we can, without great difficulties, adjust our policies on all questions standing before us, and if we are not in a position so far to provide an immediate necessary decision of this or that task . . . nevertheless, more favorable perspectives are opened. I hope that these Moscow conversations will be of some benefit from the point of view that at the future meeting of the three of us, we shall be able to adopt definite decisions on all urgent questions of our mutual interest.

Stalin's blue pencil tick upon Churchill's half-sheet of paper to the contrary notwithstanding, it is difficult to assess with certitude what, if anything, the Kremlin had hoped to achieve by the percentage agreement.

Perhaps Stalin, not unlike FDR, was more concerned with keeping his Balkan options open more than anything else, at least until the dust of the Red Army had settled. There may be more than a little irony in the judgement of one Soviet history of World War II, which noted that with the exception of Greece, 'The Red Army's successful offensive in the Southwestern theatre finally buried the plans of the British reactionary circles to forestall the Soviet military presence in the Balkans.' In this sense, Stalin's adherence to the percentage agreement would seem but part of a calculated effort in which to buy time ultimately to bury 'the plans of the British reactionary circles to forestall the Soviet military presence in the Balkans'. And who can deny that the Marshal was an expert at buying time?

Gradually informed of the thrust of the percentage agreement, though, like the principals, by no means certain of its actual meaning, President Roosevelt chose to respond to the critical joint message of his Grand Alliance partners of 10 October in muted tones. 'I am most pleased to know', he replied on 12 October, 'that you are reaching a meeting of your two minds as to international policies in which, because of our present and future common efforts to prevent international wars, we are still interested'. Politician to the core, FDR knew full well it was nearly impossible to find happy solutions for many European problems. This being so, it is hardly surprising that he would want to remain as clear of them as he could, except for those involving Germany. Domestic political considerations aside, it would seem the President revealed his thoughts most clearly when he told Harriman, in a cable dated 11 October, 'My active interest at the present time in the Balkans is that such steps as are practical should be taken to insure against the Balkans getting us into a future international war.' What practical steps Roosevelt had in mind would of necessity have to await the November elections. In the meantime, the State Department responded to the Moscow revival of spheres of influence politics with a programme of its own.

In a memorandum passed on by Under-Secretary of State Edward Stettinius to FDR on 8 November, State declared that:

> [W]hile the Government of the United States is fully aware of the existence of problems between Great Britain and the Soviet Union, this Government should not assume the attitude of supporting either country as against the other. Rather, this Government should assert the independent interest of the United States (which is also believed to be in the general interest) in favor of equitable arrangements designed to attain general peace and security on a basis of good neighborship, and should not assume the American interest requires it at this time to identify its interests with those of either the Soviet Union or Great Britain.

According to this view, American policy in the Balkans, among other places, should be governed by the following general principles: self-determination, equality of commercial opportunity, freedom of press movement and ideas, freedom for American philanthropic and educational organizations to pursue their activities on a most-favoured-nation basis, general protection of US citizens and their legitimate economic rights, and the proposition that territorial settlements should be left for postwar. However, what impression State's memorandum had on the President's thinking is unknown.

Kennan's realism

On the other side of the State Department spectrum were the views of George Frost Kennan, who at the age of 41 in 1945 was already the senior member of the American diplomatic corps in length of service in Russia. 'I am aware of the realities of this war, and of the fact that we were too weak to win it without Russia's cooperation', the minister-counsellor wrote to his friend Charles Bohlen on the eve of the Yalta Conference. 'I recognize', he continued:

> that Russia's war effort has been masterful and effective and must, to a certain extent, find its reward at the expense of other peoples in eastern and central Europe. But with all of this, I fail to see why we must associate ourselves with this political program, so hostile to the interests of the Atlantic community as a whole, so dangerous to everything which we need to see preserved in Europe. Why could we not make a decent and definite compromise with it – divide Europe frankly into spheres of influence – keep ourselves out of the Russian sphere and keep the Russians out of ours.

For Kennan, such a policy 'would have been the best thing we could do for ourselves and for our friends in Europe, and the most honest approach we could have made to the Russians'. 'Instead of this', exploded the father of containment, 'what have we done?'

> Although it was evident that the realities of the after-war were being shaped while the war was in progress we have consistently refused to

make clear what our interests and our wishes were, in eastern and central Europe. We have refused to name any limit for Russian expansion and Russian responsibilities, thereby confusing the Russians and causing them constantly to wonder whether they are asking too little or whether it was some kind of a trap. We have refused to face political issues and forced others to face them without us. We have advanced no positive, constructive program for the future of the continent: nothing that could encourage our friends, nothing that could appeal to people on the enemy's side of the line.

Though sympathetic with some of Kennan's arguments, Bohlen was quick to note that the foreign policy he spoke of could not be made in a democracy. 'Only totalitarian states', concluded Roosevelt's interpreter and recently appointed State's liaison with the Executive, 'can make and carry out such policies. Furthermore, I don't for one minute believe that there has been any time in this war when we could seriously have done very differently than we did.' Again, it is not known for certain what kind of impression such ideas had on the President's own thinking.

What is known for certain is that the subject of Balkan percentages was not again raised at the subsequent meeting of the Big Three at Yalta in February 1945, or at any other time. Militarily, the Soviet Union had further strengthened its stranglehold over Eastern and Central Europe. In the place of the October percentage agreement, the broad outlines of which were known to the Americans, the Allies, with Roosevelt at the forefront, now focused on the Declaration on Liberated Europe as the best way of dealing with the future of those countries liberated by the Red Army. Broadly speaking, the Three Powers jointly declared:

> their mutual agreement to concert during the temporary period of instability the policies of their three governments in assisting the people liberated from the domination of Nazi Germany and the peoples of the former axis satellite states to solve by democratic means their pressing political and economic problems.

Stalin's decision to sponsor unilaterally a minority government in Romania in March, not to mention continuing differences over the composition of the Polish government, suggested both to Roosevelt and the State Department that what the Kremlin really thought about was what Stalin once called 'the algebra of declarations' as opposed to 'practical arithmetic'. Stalin always preferred the latter. To Churchill, it must have appeared as nothing less than the first fruits of 'the pedantic interference of the United States' with his own preferred plans for the division of Europe. Still, the Churchill–Stalin agreements had apparently settled the future of Eastern Europe.

Conclusion

Soviet advances across the heart of Europe during the summer and autumn of 1944 sustained the power revolution that underlay the massive Soviet–German confrontation on the Eastern Front. In September, Kennan wrote from Moscow that 200 million Russians, 'united under the strong and purposeful leadership of Moscow . . . constitute a single force far greater than any other that will be left on the European continent when this war is over'. That Europe faced the most dramatic power revolution since Napoleon scarcely troubled Washington – and for good reason. The fundamental military decisions demolishing Europe's traditional equilibrium had after all been made in Berlin, not Moscow. It was Hitler's initiation of a two-front war that unloosed the forces now closing in on the Third Reich. It was the savage Nazi assault on the Soviet Union that had motivated the Kremlin's determination to prevent the recurrence of that disaster, a purpose with which few Americans cared to quarrel.

Moscow's ambitions in Eastern Europe and the Balkans expanded in response to the opportunities that flowed from the progress of Soviet arms. After 1941, the Kremlin sought essentially Western recognition of the country's annexations under the Nazi–Soviet Pact, lands to which Russia had some ethnic or historical claims.

In the absence of any restrictive agreements or countervailing power, the Soviet Union, by 1944, was free to act in accordance with its widening interests and ideological preferences. The dynamics of a changing Europe, not some expansionist blueprint, determined what occurred. The necessary Western reliance on the Soviets to deliver it from Germany was carrying a potentially heavy price. Clearly, FDR and Churchill understood that the needed Soviet victories would come with a price. They never contested the Soviet annexations under the Nazi–Soviet Pact. Nor did Roosevelt ever seriously challenge the personal diplomacy of Churchill and Stalin to divide Eastern Europe into spheres of influence.

Chapter 5
The ANZUS Treaty

The Cold War saw Australia, naturally and even automatically, on the side of America. In this sense, the traditional image of Australia as a safe ally of the United States is substantially correct. However, it implies a tendency to subservience on the side of the junior partner that generally has been conspicuously lacking. The two Pacific nations customarily have been as one on major ideological and strategic issues. Their relationship in other areas justly could be called turbulent, particularly during the tense and frustrating years of developing East–West confrontation immediately after the defeat of the Axis. The recurring collisions between Canberra and Washington in the early Cold War period did not reflect any real ideological difference between the Australian Labor government and the Truman administration. The main source of contention was paradoxically the bipartisan determination of Australian leaders to establish a binding security relationship between their country and the United States, and the equally firm and bipartisan resolve of American policymakers not to embark upon anything of the kind in the existing circumstances. Australia wanted an alliance; the United States wanted cooperation; and neither got exactly what it wanted.

9. John Curtin

A war of convenience

Strains in the relationship had been apparent even before the defeat of their common enemies. Australian Prime Minister John Curtin and Minister for External Affairs Herbert V. Evatt were appalled to discover early in 1942 that the Americans had originated the 'Atlantic First' strategy, which assigned top priority to the defeat of Germany rather than to Japan. This revelation engendered suspicions of American intentions in the Pacific that at times approximated paranoia.

Allied successes in the Pacific through 1943 gradually allayed Australian anxieties over the possibility of Japanese victory. From then on, Australian fears were concentrated on the implications of American victory. These appeared to derive some substance from statements by US Navy Secretary Frank Knox and Robert B. McCormick, editor of the *Chicago Tribune*, that after the war US security might require the control of bases in the island groups of the British Commonwealth as well as in former Japanese mandates in the Pacific. Australian concern was not allayed in the least by the assurance of Under-Secretary of State Sumner Welles that the United States had no intention of interfering with the sovereignty of the island peoples of the region. Evatt next engineered with New Zealand a joint agreement affirming that there should be no change of sovereignty affecting any of the former colonial territories south of the equator without the sanction of Canberra and Wellington. Reactions in Washington were predictably unfavourable. Secretary of State Cordell Hull ridiculed the so-called ANZAC Pact as proposing 'a Monroe Doctrine for the South Pacific', and told New Zealand Prime Minister Peter Fraser that it 'seemed to be on all four, so far as the tone and method are concerned, with the Russian action toward Great Britain'. The New Zealander agreed, thus strengthening Hull's disposition to cast Evatt as the villain of the piece. Former US Ambassador to Japan Joseph C. Grew also referred to Evatt's 'assertive leadership', and thought US policy towards territorial problems in the South Pacific should be 'chiefly to prevent the somewhat expansionist tendencies which have their roots mainly in Australia rather than in New Zealand from unduly complicating the relations of the United States with the United Kingdom, France and the Netherlands'. Consequently, each government suspected the other's ambitions.

Part of the problem undoubtedly lay in Evatt's personality. No altruistic and unequivocally Western-aligned diplomat ever succeeded in making himself more detested by the people he was most anxious to placate. Sir Alexander Cadogan, the admittedly acerbic British Under-Secretary of State for Foreign Affairs, described him as 'the most frightful man in the world', and he noted gleefully that 'everyone by now hates Evatt so much that his stock has gone down a bit and he matters less'. State Department Legal Specialist Henry Reiff warned that Evatt's presence at the United Nations 'bodes trouble' and that his arguments were only a facade to mask Australian ambitions in the region. Even Hull was impressed by Evatt's bad manners. The US representative in Canberra, Nelson T. Johnson, found the Australian minister's 'increasing megalomania' more deserving of comment. It was hardly an auspicious beginning for a close and harmonious relationship.

It was also quite misleading. Evatt was anything but anti-American in either his public policy or his private statements. He was sincere when he told Secretary of State James F. Byrnes that 'leadership by your country is the basis of the Pacific settlement'. The basic difficulty was that the Truman Administration was not prepared to assume the particular leadership role that Evatt had in mind. There were two main reasons for this. First, Evatt clearly believed that Australian–American relations should be conceived in terms of a partnership of equals with full and effective consultations on all matters of common interest. The United States was not prepared to recognize Australia as an equal partner. American policymakers were not prepared to accept the right of Australia to be consulted on issues in which no real Australian interest could be discerned. Second, and perhaps an even more serious concern, was Evatt's conviction that the United States should underwrite a formal military alliance in the Pacific, which the Americans considered to be both politically unacceptable and strategically counterproductive. Empire by invitation seldom ran smoothly.

Australian–American confrontation, therefore, was effectively guaranteed. Evatt was prepared to allow the US navy to establish a base on the island of Manus in the Australian-mandated Admiralty Group, on the condition that reciprocal facilities were made available to the Royal Australian Navy in American ports. The Americans preferred to abandon the Manus project. Evatt then demanded that the United States include in its peace treaty with Thailand a clause denying Thailand the right to enter into any international commodity arrangements unless Australia also were given the opportunity to join, and he told John R. Minter, US chargé in Canberra, that he regarded American interference in Thai affairs as an unfriendly act. Minter replied that Evatt's insistence on including the clause could be regarded as equally unfriendly. The peace settlement went through as planned. Under-Secretary of State Dean G. Acheson warned President Truman that Evatt's concept of a 'US-Australia-New Zealand joint defense scheme analogous to the US-Canada joint defense scheme' should be resolutely opposed as being 'premature, inadvisable and likely to encourage the USSR to advocate similar over-all arrangements elsewhere not to the advantage of the United Nations or the US'. To make sure that Evatt's opportunities to push this particular barrow himself in Washington would be limited, Acting Chief of Protocol Stanley Woodward advised that requests by the Australian Minister for External Affairs for an audience with Truman should not be overly encouraged. 'If an appointment is made', he wrote stiffly, 'the Department hopes very much that it will be at the convenience of the President rather than at Mr Evatt's'.

On 8 July 1946, Acheson agreed that the two countries should establish full ambassadorial relations as 'the natural consequence of the increasingly close and cordial relations between Australia and the United States'. However, the choice of appointees to the new positions served to illuminate the highly asymmetrical nature of the relationship. Richard G. Casey had been the first Australian Minister in Washington in 1941. One of the most experienced of Australian diplomats, Sir Frederic Eggleston, had held the post since 1945. The new ambassador, Norman J. Makin, was a former minister, a speaker of the House of Representatives, and the first President of the Security Council. By contrast, the first US ambassador to Australia, Robert Butler, was a businessman who had held his only previous official post 30 years before. He had then been deputy governor of Mindanao. Drew Pearson categorized him as 'one of the most well-meaning but left-handed of American Ambassadors'. He certainly seemed incredibly unaware of what was expected of him on ceremonial occasions, opening an exhibition of paintings, including works by the Duchess of Gloucester, with the brief speech: 'I like art; this is it.'

Butler nevertheless appears to have been popular in Australia. Not even the most adept ambassador could have done much to compensate for Evatt's unfailing skill in enraging his American colleagues. Another bitter wrangle soon developed over the decision of the Supreme Commander for the Allied Powers (SCAP) to authorize a Japanese whaling expedition to the Antarctic during the 1946–7 season. Evatt claimed that the decision had been taken unilaterally by SCAP, with no prior consultation with interested Allied governments such as Australia. George Atcheson, Jr, US political adviser in Japan, claimed that in fact there had been at least prior notification of the SCAP decision and that Evatt's statement was therefore dishonest in its implications. In any case, Atcheson told Secretary of State George C. Marshall that:

Australian distorted pronouncements and unwarranted criticisms have been so violent and so widely publicized in the Far East that,

US decisions having been made and announced, question has resolved itself into one of upholding prestige of US in Japan and throughout Far East.... It is the opinion here of those closely familiar with Australian political scene that Australian protesters flow from policy of endeavouring by loud assertion to bring Australia to place of effective predominance in the Far East ... any appeasement of the Australians will without question seriously undermine American prestige in this part of the world.

The Pacific Basin

Australia and the United States once again appeared to be not so much partners in peace as rivals bitterly contending for the domination of the Pacific Basin. The contest obviously could not be a serious one. However, what was intensely serious in American eyes was the extent to which Australian intransigence was jeopardizing the effective implementation of Cold War grand strategy. On 8 May 1947, in a speech heralding the Marshall Plan, Acheson had linked Japan with Germany as 'two of the greatest workshops of Europe and Asia, upon whose production Europe and Asia were to an important degree dependent before the war', but which 'have hardly been able even to begin the process of reconstruction because of the lack of a peace settlement'.

The main impediment to the conclusion of a peace settlement with Japan was Evatt's commitment to a tough policy towards that country, ultimately involving the destruction of Japan's capacity to wage war, which logically would entail the substantial restriction and supervision of Japan's industrial recovery. The memory of the Japanese threat to the very existence of Australia was fresh. Evatt refused to accept an American invitation to attend a conference on 19 August 1947 to discuss the formulation of a draft peace settlement with Japan. He instead set up his own conference in Canberra for 26 August. An open breach appeared to have been deliberately programmed, but Evatt was consistent in his unpredictability. He visited General MacArthur in Tokyo in July and apparently was converted to the American position with respect to Japan, assuring the sceptical Atcheson on his departure that 'his desire was that the British Commonwealth cooperate with the United States to the fullest in conjunction with Japan'. In the meantime, back in Canberra, he told the bewildered Australian journalists that he and SCAP 'found ourselves in agreement on the steps to be undertaken in negotiating the Japanese Peace Treaty, on the main principles which should be contained in it, and also on the possible lines of the supervisory machinery which should be established under the Treaty'. The Australian media could cope with this apparent reversal of attitude on Evatt's part only by suggesting that the Minister had discovered that General MacArthur all along had been following Australian policies.

There certainly could be no doubt, as State Department official Robert A. Lovett told Truman, that a serious gap between the two countries seemed to have been closed as a result of Evatt's visit to Tokyo, and that 'he and General Macarthur got along famously'. Nor was there any possible doubt that Evatt had every desire to get along famously with President Truman. He assured the President that he was a devoted friend and admirer, lauded him for his 'own innate strength which is stronger because of your humanity and your consideration at all times for the toilers and the underprivileged', claimed that 'no sane man can doubt your complete devotion to the cause of peace and the betterment of all mankind', and concluded with the rather surprising news that Ambassador Butler 'had won the confidence and friendship of all sections of this community'. Truman could have done no less under the circumstances than reply that he believed that it was 'essential that Australia and the United States be on the friendliest terms', and that he hoped that Evatt would make it a point always to come and see him when he was in the United States, a hope that his advisers obviously were determined should be fulfilled as seldom as possible.

Evatt could only hope for the best. In one of his last ministerial speeches, he stressed the need for 'the maintenance of our special relationship with the United States of America', with which he considered Australia to be on terms of 'close and cordial comradeship'. By contrast, the Americans could see nothing but trouble ahead, so long as Evatt remained Minister for External Affairs. Lovett had warned Truman earlier about Evatt's 'aggressive, egocentric manner and blunt address in debate and personal relations', and he felt that 'it is not always clear whether he is motivated by true patriotism or simply by egotism'. A State Department policy paper noted grimly that 'the Australian attitude towards the Indonesian decolonization conflict is not helpful to our efforts to obtain a satisfactory conclusion. . . . To the extent that this attitude on the part of Australia serves to weaken the democratic front, it has and will prove embarrassing to us.' Secretary of Defense James V. Forrestal recorded in similar terms that 'Evatt, who is President of the General Assembly, is an active source of both irritation and uncertainty. The result of his activities . . . has been greatly to undermine the American position among the neutral nations.'

Even the CIA found the Australian Labor government to be soft on communism and noted for future reference that Evatt's brother had been the president of a communist-front organization in New South Wales. The US chargé in Canberra, Andrew B. Foster, believed that Evatt's 'highly academic approach to international problems' would continue to lead to 'an almost automatic opposition to United States proposals and policies in connection with the future of Japan', and that the Labor government as a whole was 'extremely jealous of the independent position of Australia, suspicious of what it regards as American economic imperialism, and determined not to be pushed around', while at the same time continuing to share with the Australian people 'the complacent assumption that when the next war comes, if it does, the United States will bail them out just as it did last time'.

It appeared that Australia expected to enjoy all the advantages of being an ally without undertaking any of the responsibilities.

Relations scarcely were improved by still another inauspicious US ambassadorial appointment. Myron M. Cowen, lawyer and businessman, had devoted his stint in Canberra between July 1948 and March 1949 mainly to resolving problems of double taxation between Australia and the United States. This in itself would not have aroused much hostility on either side of the Atlantic, but Evatt's sensibilities were outraged when Cowen was transferred on his own request to the Philippines before completing his normal tour of duty in Australia. Evatt's attempts to block his transfer appear to have inspired Cowen to foster Philippine interests at the expense of Australia. Australian Immigration Minister Arthur A. Calwell was amazed to find himself being accused by Cowen in Manila of pursuing 'a private feud with the Philippines'. Evatt might have been even more amazed, as well as enraged, to discover that Cowen had been, on his account, 'entirely responsible' for moves to have him replaced as President of the General Assembly by Filipino Carlos P. Romulo. He presumably would have been more upset had he known that Truman had decided to give the post in Canberra to defeated Alabama Congressman Pete Jarman, who had applied for it simply because he needed the money. 'Since I really need to go on the payroll', Jarman appealed, 'I will very much appreciate your expediting my appointment in any way possible'. Some of Truman's supporters did not think that Jarman merited such a handout, although they agreed that Canberra was a suitable place of exile for him. 'I see you have nominated former Rep. Pete Jarman, of Alabama, as Ambassador to Australia', the international trustee of the International Woodworkers of America wrote to Truman. 'That I am sorry to hear. We worked hard here to defeat him, as he was no friend to your program or Labor's, but again it may be wise if you were able to nominate several of the Rep's from the South to posts in some faraway places.' Indeed, it might have seemed that Washington was not placing high priority on improving its relations with the Australian Labor government.

The Truman Administration, however, actually was counting on the early departure of the Labor government, taking Evatt with it. Conciliation or even cooperation effectively had been abandoned, and Australian diplomats were confronted with the alarming spectacle of Acheson at his conciliatory worst. Ambassador Makin approached the Secretary in September 1949, apologetically presenting a typically 'urgent' message from Evatt, expressing the Minister's disturbance at learning that discussions had taken place in Washington regarding Far Eastern matters without the participation of an Australian representative. Acheson was furious. The message was 'most surprising... it would be quite impossible for the United States to undertake that it would discuss no matter affecting the Far East except in the presence of a representative from Australia'. Evatt was 'to be under no illusion about the matter but to understand that we would continue to proceed as we had'. Assistant Secretary of State for Far Eastern Affairs W. Walton Butterworth urged in similar terms that the United States 'should not accede to any request from Australia at this time to provide a security guarantee', if Evatt were to renew his appeal for a Pacific pact as the price for Australian concurrence in American proposals for a peace settlement with Japan. Dominion Affairs Officer J. Harold Shullaw suggested on the eve of the Australian federal elections that 'a Conservative Government would be less inclined to be demagogic and would tend to be more reasonable and less unsympathetic to the United States point of view'. On election day, Ambassador Jarman even wrote to Richard G. Casey, federal President of the Liberal party, congratulating him in advance on his party's defeat of Labor. It was an interesting return for all of Evatt's expressions of good will for the Democrats.

Evatt's absence only could make the course of Australian–American relations more harmonious. Washington, however, had not taken full account of what it might be confronted with in his stead. James Plimsoll, a member of the Australian delegation on the Far Eastern Commission, visited his old friend, John M. Allison, director of the Office of Northeast Asian Affairs, to warn him that while the new Australian government 'would wish to go as far as possible in cooperating with the United States on Japanese matters', he was 'certain that such cooperation could be made easier if some sort of definite defense arrangements could be concluded regarding the Pacific between the United States and Australia'. Evatt might have passed into the shadows of the opposition, but his policies were still in the foreground.

In fact, they had acquired a new protagonist who was in many ways far more formidable than Evatt himself. Nobody ever suggested that the new Australian Minister for External Affairs, Sir Percy C. Spender, possessed Evatt's philosophical breadth and intellectual vision, but no one denied that he possessed other qualities more appropriate to the diplomatic arena. Originally, he planned a career as a professional athlete, but he decided instead to practise law, where his treatment of hostile witnesses earned him the admiring, if unaffectionate, sobriquet of 'the butcher bird'. His skills were exhibited in his first weeks as minister when he railroaded a series of proposals on economic cooperation through a Commonwealth foreign ministers' conference in Colombo, in January 1950. Opposition was put to flight by simply leaking to the Sydney press a story denouncing the 'disposition in powerful quarters to let things go for the time being . . . a continuation of the wartime thinking of putting Europe first and letting Asia wait'.

The search for collective security

One particular lesson that Spender learned at Colombo was that the Commonwealth in itself was not an appropriate basis on which to erect a structure of collective security. The question of a Pacific defence pact was, he claimed, 'in this manner, deliberately raised, in order to be dismissed'. Accordingly, on 9 March 1950, he tuned his song to American ears in a speech that insisted on the need for urgent short-term measures to confront the 'consolidation of Communism in China and the evident threat of its emergence as a growing force throughout South and South East Asia'. Efforts to 'stabilize governments and to create conditions of economic life and living standards under which the false ideological attractions which Communism excites will lose its [sic] force' would be 'essentially long term measures'. In the meantime, it would be necessary that 'all governments who are directly interested in the preservation of peace throughout South and South East Asia, and in the advancement of human welfare under the democratic system should consider immediately whether some form of regional pact for common defense is a practical possibility'.

Circumstances played much more favourably into Spender's hands than into those of Evatt. On 24 June, the US ambassador in Seoul, John Muccio, reported 'a heavy attack, different from patrol forays that had occurred in the past', amounting, in his opinion, to 'an all-out offensive against the Republic of Korea'. Keith C. Shann, the Australian representative in the United Nations acting on Spender's instructions, asked immediately what we could do in the way of meeting force with force. He thought perhaps the Australians were in a position to help if the United Nations decided to take strong action. Squadron 77 of the Royal Australian Air Force was already on stand-by in Japan, being under the operational control of the 5th US Air Force. On 29 June, these aircraft, along with the destroyer *Bataan* and the frigate *Shoalhaven*, were formally offered to Acheson. On the morning of 2 July, Mustangs of Squadron 77 were in action, strafing North Korean T-34s and occasionally South Korean forces heading in the same direction. The Australians were not exactly the first to make a positive offer of assistance, but they were the first actually to get into the fight.

Spender had another alternative. On 30 June, Truman decided to send US ground troops into action in Korea. The Joint Chiefs of Staff considered that 'Australia is capable of furnishing three infantry battalions . . . and that such a contribution from Australia is highly desirable'. Australian Prime Minister Robert G. Menzies decided to visit London to consult with the British government before determining Australian policy. He was told that the British were in accord with his own decision not to commit troops. With Menzies halfway across the Atlantic, the British then decided to send their own force. Spender was apprised of British intentions by Australian diplomat Sir Alan Watt. The Minister immediately proceeded to bully Acting Prime Minister Sir Arthur Fadden into issuing, on his authority and without consulting either Menzies or other ministers, a statement written by Spender, to the effect that the Australian government had decided to provide ground troops for use in Korea in response to the appeal of the United Nations. Spender's timing was perfect. His highly unorthodox announcement actually was made simultaneously with that of the British government. Australia had finally made it to the head of the Commonwealth queue.

Spender was now looking for a *quid pro quo*. Menzies, under British influence, was opposed totally to the idea of a Pacific pact, from which most other Commonwealth countries would be necessarily excluded. He told Fadden to warn Spender that the project was 'not on the map' and referred to it himself as 'a superstructure on a foundation of jelly'. This had no effect on the 'butcher bird'. Spender told the annual conference of the New South Wales Division of the Liberal party on 4 August that 'consultation between Members of the British Commonwealth is not always satisfactory or effective'. Accordingly, the Australian government maintained that

> since it came into office in December last [it had] placed special emphasis upon its desire for the closest relation with the United States. . . . What has taken place in Korea is indicative of the close association which we have endeavoured to create. It would be the purpose of the Australian Government to make those ties closer still, so that, on both sides of the Pacific, there will be two nations understanding each other, who will be able to work with the other

democracies in the area for the purpose of bringing stability to this part of the world.

He was even more specific in an address to the nation on the eve of his departure for London and Washington. He proclaimed that

> Australia must seek to revive the close working association with our American friends which existed during the war. This relationship should, in due course, be given formal expression within the framework of a Pacific Pact.

Spender still had to persuade the Americans, and he cleverly decided to try the candid approach when he met with President Truman. He explained that a Pacific pact would be meaningless unless the United States were a party to it, but that he had failed completely to make any headway at all in his discussions on this issue with other Commonwealth governments. Truman agreed to discuss it with Secretary Acheson, who did not immediately warm to Spender. The Secretary briefly told Spender that he could not conceive of Australia's being subject to hostile attack, or US failure to provide aid. Apart from that, Acheson merely delivered

> generalities directed to the difficulties of any regional security arrangement . . . and the great differences which existed between the North Atlantic groups of nations and those of the western Pacific and Asia. This was becoming a familiar refrain.

Special Representative John Foster Dulles was even more uncompromising when Spender met with him at Flushing Meadows to discuss the Japanese peace treaty. Dulles began by confronting Spender, without any preliminaries, with the most extreme and uncompromising version of the American position, presenting him with a document that omitted any reference at all to limitations on Japanese freedom to rearm. Spender was having none of it. He told Dulles that Australia never would accept such a treaty, and he did not regard Dulles's proposal that the United States should retain

10. John Foster Dulles

troops in Japan as providing the slightest security for Australia; the only solution was a Pacific pact. Dulles stated that Spender's fears of Japan were exaggerated, to which Spender replied that Dulles's objections were illusory. Dulles nonetheless agreed that a compromise solution would have to be found.

The compromise agreed on in further discussions on 30 October among Spender, Dulles, and Dean Rusk amounted virtually to the acceptance in principle of the Australian proposal. Referring to a draft approved by Rusk, Spender told the federal parliament in Canberra that he

> had found in the United States that a most genuine friendship exists towards Australia and Australians . . . there is no doubt, at this moment, that this warm-hearted nation would immediately and effectively come to our aid in the event of an act of aggression against Australia. But it is not a one-way traffic in obligations with which Australia is concerned. . . . What we desire is a permanent regional basis of collective security, constructed in accordance with the United Nations Charter, which has as its pivotal point some obligation comparable to that set forth in Article 5 of the North Atlantic Treaty – namely, that an armed attack upon one shall be deemed an armed attack upon all. We desire to see formal machinery set up to which, amongst others, the United States of America and ourselves are parties, which will enable us effectively to plan the use of our resources and military power.

The Korean War

Spender's desires might have remained unrealized except that the United States was in urgent need of a reliable ally, as Chinese forces had entered the Korean War on 25 October. British Foreign Secretary Ernest Bevin flatly stated that he could not endorse the US suggestion that the Chinese intervention might necessitate the violation of the Manchurian border by UN forces. By contrast, Spender urged that it should be made clear within the Security Council that it would be unreasonable and militarily disadvantageous for UN forces to continue indefinitely to observe restraint. He warned Australians that the Soviets were using China to do their work for them in pursuit of a long-term plan to dominate the world. He stressed that under such circumstances, 'we must permit nothing to prevent the free peoples, in particular the British people, standing steadfast with the United States of America in the difficulties that confront us'. These protestations of support helped the Joint Chiefs of Staff to reach the decision that the State Department should explore at the earliest opportunity the possibilities of a Pacific pact with Australia. The Joint Chiefs, however, were not prepared to contemplate the prospect of having an Australian military mission arrive in Washington to discuss specifics with them. They strongly believed that,

> from the military point of view, any possible advantages to be gained as a result of inviting the Australian Government to send a high level military mission to Washington would be transitory and, in all probability, negligible; on the other hand, they perceive serious and far-reaching military disadvantages in having such a group in Washington, particularly in light of the present and projected status of the United States planning for a global war.

However, it was becoming increasingly difficult to ignore Australian approaches. Spender was in full flight again. A US resolution in the Security Council on 20 January 1951, which denounced the Chinese for being engaged themselves in aggression in Korea, was drafted substantially by Shann on Spender's instructions, despite the fact that Menzies himself was counselling caution on directions from London. The Melbourne *Age*, noting Shann's frequent shifts of position depending on whether Menzies or Spender had gotten to him last, asked: 'Is our new policy to be one of saying "yes" to whatever emanates from Washington?' As far as Spender was concerned, it was to be the policy until at least a Pacific pact had been signed; victory was in his hands. His influence had succeeded in producing, according to Sir Alan Watt, a degree of cordiality in Australian–American relations that had not been known since the days of the Pacific War. Spender's efforts in this direction undoubtedly were made easier by the lack of effective parliamentary opposition, except indeed from his own Prime Minister. Bipartisanship in the true sense scarcely was to be looked for in the Australian political climate, but the Labor party was providing at least indirect support by denouncing, with perfect justice, the decidedly limited nature of Australian military support in Korea. Labor leader Joseph B. Chifley asserted that 'it was not a matter of what sort of government operated in North or South Korea. The thing that mattered was that a country had been ruthlessly and wantonly attacked contrary to the principles of the Charter.'

However, there was still a long road to travel. Menzies remained loathe to alienate the British. Dulles arrived in Canberra on 14 February for talks with the Australians and New Zealanders, and was ready to pretend that the issue of a Pacific pact had never been raised in connection with that of a Japanese peace treaty. Spender informed him promptly that the Australian government never would accept a treaty such as Dulles was proposing without accompanying arrangements to ensure Australian security. Menzies himself urged Spender not to press too hard for a tripartite defence pact, for fear of jeopardizing the chances of at least a presidential guarantee of Australia and New Zealand. But the 'butcher bird' knew with whom he was dealing. Dulles finally admitted that he had intended to discuss a Pacific pact all along. After three more days of vehement wrangling, the three delegations agreed on a draft security treaty, which represented, with marginal changes, the text of the final ANZUS Pact.

Australian attitudes towards the United States had not changed fundamentally with the change of government in Canberra. Evatt had sought an alliance with the United States as earnestly as Percy Spender. The difference was simply that Evatt's attempts had failed and Spender's had succeeded. Also, circumstances had favoured Spender and not Evatt. Spender was unquestionably a more adept operator, but all the tactical skill in the world would have been unavailing against the ironbound intransigence of Acheson and Dulles, had not the Chinese intervention in Korea made it urgently desirable for the United Slates to conclude a peace settlement with Japan without positively estranging its

11. The signing of ANZUS in San Francisco, 1951

vociferous supporter in the South Pacific. In this sense, Mao Zedong was the real godfather of ANZUS; nevertheless, the bipartisan element in Australian policy cannot be overstressed. It was rock solid. Spender deliberately aligned himself with the United States wherever possible, while Evatt appeared, at least in Washington, to be doing exactly the opposite. However, Spender's chase had an end in view. The ANZUS Pact finally was pried out of Washington despite the misgivings of the State Department and the firm resolve of the Joint Chiefs to keep contacts with the Australians and New Zealanders on defence matters as superficial as possible.

The ANZUS – or the Australian–New Zealand–US Security Treaty – was signed in San Francisco on 1 September 1951, ratified by President Truman on 15 April 1952, and entered into force two weeks later, on 29 April. Conceived in close connection with the conclusion of a so-called 'soft' Japanese peace treaty, and contrary to historical charges of subservience on the side of the junior partner, the ANZUS alliance was negotiated only after much tough bargaining. The main source of contention was, paradoxically, the bipartisan determination of Australian leaders to establish a binding security relationship between their country and the United States, and the equally firm and bipartisan resolve of American policymakers not to embark upon anything of the kind. Put simply, Canberra wanted strategic reassurance that America would come to Australia's aid in its next time of troubles; Washington wanted cooperation, an opportunity to take advantage of Australia's unique geographical position in the western Pacific, as well as the overall political position in Southeast Asia. Neither got exactly what it wanted, Australia's future leaders reserving the right to see the alliance a little differently from the way the United States saw it. In any case, 'for the decision-makers in Canberra', recalled historian Coral Bell, who was in the Department of External Affairs at the time, 'the original interpretation . . . was that the rationale of the treaty should be seen as 90 per cent security blanket against revival of Japanese ambitions in the Pacific, and 10 per cent insurance policy against possible future Chinese expansionism'. Asia would always be a dangerous place for Australia without America's strategic engagement.

Conclusion

Australia's relations with the United States could never be more than paradoxical. On the one hand, nothing could be more natural than a close relationship between these two continental, British-begotten, frontier-shaped powers, both vitally concerned with international security, and with striking cultural and political similarities. On the other hand, any diplomatic relationship that did develop between them could only perforce be asymmetrical. Since the last decades of the 19th century, the United States could normally count on at least fifteen times the population and nineteen times the economic resources of Australia. This huge disparity in power had one inevitable consequence: in any diplomatic partnership, the United States was always going to be vastly more important to Australia than Australia to the United States. In this sense, then, the ANZUS Treaty can be seen as a triumph of Australian diplomacy.

Chapter 6
Diplomacy in the age of globalization

It is a truism – but none the less for that – diplomacy in the age of globalization has become something very much more than the diplomacy of states and governments. It might be urged that it is still true that the legal formalities based on the 1961 Vienna Convention on Diplomatic Relations acknowledge only the diplomacy of states. Nor can one deny that the entire apparatus of traditional diplomacy is alive and well. It is relevant, indeed. This apparatus includes extensive consular networks sustained by the problems associated with the huge and continuing movement of peoples which is, doubtless, one of the salient features of our times, as well as the humanitarian disasters that impact the daily media. At another level, states have found themselves forced to alter their practice of diplomacy, both institutionally and in its external focus. The most commonly observed results of both of these have been the reduction of representation – for example, Australia has one-fifth fewer diplomats now than in 1996 – the constant financial crises the diplomatic services face, the ever-presence of anxious discussions about what state diplomacy is now actually for, and the consequential emergence of the doctrines of 'public diplomacy' (see Chapter 1).

On the ground, though, it is impossible to ignore the diplomacy of the global economic system, ranging from the activities of the TNCs (transnational corporations) to the interventions of the global economic IGOs (intergovernmental organizations), particularly the World Trade Organization, a relatively new IGO established as a result of the Uruguay Round of trade negotiations in the late 1980s, under the aegis of the GATT (General Agreement on Tariffs and Trade) process. These all have important diplomatic webs which operate both within and outside the traditional diplomatic system. The same is true of another vast area of diplomatic activity, the diplomacy of civil society organizations – though there is a shrinking minority of observers who regard them as a category error. In any case, the saga of failed and failing states, civil conflict, and international terrorism has created an entirely new global world of urgent communications between states and NGOs (non-governmental organizations), between NGOs and IGOs, and amongst NGOs themselves. The remarks that follow will attempt to describe the context in which these entities function.

A defining feature of 21st-century globalization is the increasing complexity of global relations and the rapidity with which information ricochets around the world, opening up new avenues for the conduct of diplomacy, while helping new participants to become involved. Globalization has rendered the world more sensitive to sudden financial or strategic shocks, however localized they might at first appear. The great financial crisis that arose in 2008, with costs passed on to the next generation of the world's taxpayers, said it all.

Equally important, the shifting terrain of global relations virtually ensures that security issues of any kind can appear unexpectedly and can rapidly change in shape and scope. Human security risks can usefully be thought of as 'polymorphous', in that, at any one moment in time, people and their communities can be subject to political violence, or environmental scarcities, which, individually, can generate a host of future dangers: food shortages, economic hardship, crime, disease, and human rights abuses. To define a security crisis as military, environmental, societal, or financial is to downplay the 'strings' or 'threads' of interconnected happenings, decisions, ideas, and beliefs that shape trajectories of risk.

Complex crises

Human security crises 'cluster' around interconnected domains of risk, though there are always problems. In the arbitrary categorization of risks, for example, human security risk analysis tends to falter without an appreciation of the dynamics of the interactions between risk factors. Drug trafficking creates a temporal linkage between the fates of communities in the developed and developing worlds, even if the numbers of persons involved is quite small. According to the UN Office of Drug Control (UNODC), over a 12-month period spanning 2005/6, an estimated 200 million persons used drugs illegally out of a global population of 6.475 billion. Of these, 110 million used drugs on a monthly basis, of whom 25 million, or 0.6% of the global working-age population (15–64), were classed as 'problem drug users'. Yet the total annual US drug control budget stood at US \$12.5 billion in 2004, more than four times the value of total US contributions to the United Nations. This is a measure of the scale of the drug 'problem' in the USA which extends far beyond the number of addicts to the corrosive influence of traffickers and the webs of criminal activity that envelop the addicted. Corruption in police ranks and among government officials corrodes law enforcement and public confidence in government institutions. At the regional level, drug production in Latin America destabilizes legitimate governments and creates *de facto* 'narco states' in territory beyond central government control.

According to World Health Organization statistics, over 57 million people died from preventable diseases in 2006, more disease-related deaths in one year than the combined total of combat deaths in two world wars. UNAIDS estimates 33 million people worldwide are infected with the human immunodeficiency virus

(HIV), with the vast majority located in sub-Saharan Africa, which accounts for 22.5 million, or 68%, of all infections. Of those diagnosed with the virus, only a small proportion have succumbed to acquired immunodeficiency syndrome (AIDS), in which the immune system is gradually destroyed. Two million people died from HIV/AIDS in 2006, just over 1% of all disease-related deaths. But while diseases such as tuberculosis, cholera, and malaria can be treated, the virus that causes AIDS can be arrested with antiretroviral drugs (ARVs), but remains – for the present – incurable. The search for a 'cure' involves not just the pursuit of a wonder drug that can destroy the virus but the reshaping of socio-economic environments in which the virus is known to thrive.

Conflict, in addition to its political, social, economic, and even cultural roots, can also be linked to radical changes in the natural environment. According to Jared Diamond, the underlying causes of the Rwandan genocide, which claimed the lives of an estimated 800,000 people in 1994, were land degradation and attendant population pressures which destabilized Rwandan society. Resource scarcity is likely to increase, and with it the likelihood of environmental refugees moving *en masse* across international boundaries.

Former World Bank economist Nicholas Stern lays out an alarming global scenario on the potential economic and social impacts of climate change. Synthesizing scientific data on climate change, Stern calibrates a sliding scale of natural and human disasters arising from the warming of the Earth's atmosphere. A worst-case scenario was predicated on a 5-degree Celsius increase in the Earth's temperature causing sea levels to rise, extensive inundation of low-lying coastal areas, and widespread water stress threatening food security in India and China – effectively one-third of the world's population – with obvious consequences for economic and political security at the regional and global levels. While these scenarios are increasingly accepted as plausible in even the most sceptical quarters, remedial steps have proved difficult to coordinate at the global level.

Approaching human security

As the Commission on Human Security argues in its 2003 Report, conflict prevention, disease eradication, poverty alleviation, sustainable economic development, food security, and the promotion of human rights are interlinked security concerns. The scope of human security so defined fitted well with objectives outlined in the UN's Millennium Development Goals (MDGs).

Set forth at the 2000 Millennium Summit, these MDGs are *inter alia*:

i)   eradicate poverty and hunger,

ii)   achieve universal primary education,

iii) promote gender equity and empower women,

iv)   reduce child mortality,

v)   improve maternal health,

vi)   arrest the spread of HIV/AIDS, malaria, and other diseases,

vii) promote environmental sustainability, and

viii) develop a global partnership for development.

Indicative of the careful structuring of the UN's message, these goals were grouped for rhetorical effect by Secretary-General Kofi Annan (1996–2006) to resonate with the ideals of Woodrow Wilson and Franklin D. Roosevelt.

Although presented in the neutral language of public policy, each of these goals, in order to be achieved, requires that significant local cultural and political challenges be overcome. The MDGs rest on an overwhelming empirical case made by Amartya Sen as to the critical importance to human wellbeing of education, health

12. Kofi Annan

care, gender equity, economic opportunity, and respect
for human rights.

The achievement of gender equity is today widely regarded as
pivotal to sustainable human development. 'Women's agency',
where permitted in the development process, leads to the more
effective utilization of natural and human resources, because
women tend to ensure that resources introduced into the
community are shared equitably and that development lessons are
learned and passed on to the next generation. And yet gender
equity advocates confront strong opposition in societies in which
women are barred from higher levels of education and from
joining the professions. In many parts of the world, 'traditional
values' are used to justify such exclusion of women. This is not a

question of religious conservatism versus secular modernity. In many modern Islamic countries, Malaysia being a good example, young women comprise a majority of tertiary students. Rather, it is a question of entrenched custom, patriarchal dominance, and economic underdevelopment – systemic factors that can take decades to break down.

According to Roland Paris, the sheer scope of issues encompassed by the UN's broad conception of human security carries the risk of being too cumbersome to serve as an operational definition. Narrowing their focus, researchers at the Canadian Human Security Centre at the University of British Columbia, in their *Human Security Report 2006*, limit the scope of human security to the study of the 'incidence, severity, causes and consequences of global violence'. Placing human security squarely within the orbit of conflict studies, their approach attached greatest importance to humanitarian assistance for victims of war and to the conditions that promote peace within and between states. Paradoxically, and unintentionally, they ensure that war remains at the top of the international security agenda. Further, by narrowing our focus to the immediate causes and consequences of conflict, we lose sight of the long-term trajectories of risk that can culminate in societal collapse.

Limiting definitions of war and conflict to statistical criteria also distorts our reading of the 'health' of the contemporary global system. According to data provided by Swedish researchers, the scale or intensity of conflict differs from that of war in the annual number of 'battle-related deaths'; 25 battle-related deaths per year, including civilian casualties, for political violence to be categorized as armed conflict, and 1,000 combatant and non-combatant battle-related deaths per year for political violence to be categorized as a war. Applying these criteria, researchers have claimed that the incidence of war is declining and that, consequently, the world is becoming a safer place. However, shots do not need to be exchanged for the conditions of war or armed conflict to exist. In order to assess the potential for political violence to erupt and to escalate into war, we need to appreciate the diverse reasons why people resort to violence and why states make war on each other. Rather than concentrate upon the immediacy of violence and its consequences, we should look to the 'early warning signs' of conflict or war, in an effort to limit the resort to political violence.

In 'latent conflict' situations, a ceasefire, or even a formal treaty, might well exist between rival parties but the grievances and suspicions that ignited political violence have yet to subside. Indian and Pakistani troops stare at each other across the disputed line of division in Kashmir, occasionally exchanging shells and rifle shot, while militant groups sponsored by each of the sides engage in terrorist violence on both sides of the border. In Sri Lanka, a 2001 ceasefire between the government and the Tamil Tigers, fighting for an independent homeland in the north and east of the island state, broke down in 2005 when both parties resumed their 20-year struggle. Ironically, while the ceasefire remains theoretically intact, an estimated 7,000 people have since died in renewed fighting. Instances of periodic but persistent deadly violence can be found throughout Africa, Asia, and Latin America.

The security spectrum

For a definition of human security to have explanatory force, and to appeal to decision-makers and researchers alike, it must establish a conceptual link with notions of world order. To put it another way, decision-makers need the intellectual equipment and disposition to see the 'full spectrum' of security to identify security risks and preventive measures that do not escalate into the use of force. Further, to be serviceable at a policy level, such a definition must be anchored to a realization of the limitations imposed by an imperfect 'anarchic' inter-state system. This inevitably leads to compromises in the prioritization of human security issues – and to tensions between those disposed towards morality and ethics in international affairs and those who see the world in terms of power politics.

Human security was presaged in the policies of small to medium powers. Without employing the term, the Australian government, for example, incorporated a prototypical human security framework into Australian foreign and defence policy in the late 1980s. The 1989 *Statement on Australia's Regional Security* drew attention to the interconnections between traditional and non-traditional risks confronting Australia and the Asian region, from underdevelopment, to drug trafficking, to HIV/AIDS. Importantly, the policy prescription envisaged a positive 'mulitidmensional' response incorporating military, diplomatic, economic, and technical cooperation, thus linking Australian security to the security of Australia's immediate neighbours. More recently, Canada adopted an explicit and comprehensive human security agenda, as did Japan and other member states of the Human Security Network. Encompassing institutional, individual, and systemic considerations, Canada defines human security in broad terms as:

> ... in essence, an effort to construct a global society where the safety of the individual is at the centre of international priorities and a motivating force for international action; where international humanitarian standards and the rule of law are advanced and woven into a coherent web protecting the individual; where those who violate these standards are held fully accountable; and where our global, regional and bilateral institutions – present and future – are built and equipped to enhance and enforce these standards.

System-level governance

In shifting the locus of security away from states and the pursuit of military power to the security of people or individuals, the human security debate opens opportunities for a more comprehensive and flexible definition of security in which local and global levels of analysis are distinguished. Even if, as globalization theory maintains, place is diminishing in its significance as global economic relations transcend 'time and space', attachments to place, identity, and nation remain salient and potent realities. In 1945, five states – Britain, the USA, China, the USSR, and France – set the agenda for the United Nations Organization. As of 2008, there were 192 UN member states out of a total 207 nation-states worldwide. The five permanent members still wield enormous influence, but they must do so in a more complex environment in which attachments to national political space, real or imagined, have not subsided.

According to Jim Whitman, 'the weight of evidence is that our capacity to produce unwanted and sometimes dangerous conditions on a global scale is running greatly in excess of our deliberative and control mechanisms'. Human societies are 'manufacturing' new global security risks at a faster rate than existing institutions can cope. Adopting the language of neo-liberal management, Annan argued that the new millennium thus needed a new method of global problem-solving, one which placed emphasis upon 'integration', 'coherence', 'flexibility', and 'informational capacity' across government, non-governmental, and intergovernmental sectors. Institutional reform and reforms to international rules were essential to the pursuit of human security.

The UN's millennium goals established policy priorities for the international community, but their realization depends upon the mobilization of institutions and people. Human security cannot be achieved without firm economic and political foundations to support the realization of basic needs and which offer more than just the promise that aspirations for a better life lie within reach of 'ordinary' people. Between the individual and the international community stand states that may or may not hold the wellbeing of their citizens as a paramount national interest and either persecute or make war against them. In the absence of a global sovereign, the advancement of a human security agenda requires international interventions ranging from development assistance to the deployment of peacekeepers. Governance thus becomes the challenge of brokering 'solutions' to a dazzling array of security challenges.

In the absence of a genuinely participatory system of global government, states alone offer the tangible prospect for the kind of liberal democracy lauded by those who decry the state for meddling in economic affairs. Effective national-level governance is an essential complement to the advancement of human security, but, as the Commission for Africa recognized, African underdevelopment is a direct consequence of governmental failures spanning 40 years. The 'weakness of government and the absence of an effective state', so it concluded, was manifest in the 'inability of government and the public services to create the right economic, social and legal framework which will encourage economic growth and allow poor people to participate in it'.

Similarly, the cosmopolitan ideal of a world without political boundaries can only be realized with some other political machinery by which decisions can be made and differences resolved at the local and global levels. States remain the essential building-blocks of global order, and there are serious questions as to whether the dynamics of inter-state relations have evolved to the extent that military forces can be decommissioned. While power is becoming more diffuse in the international system, and governance networks more sophisticated and extensive, people and states continue to pursue or wield power for the most self-interested and nefarious of purposes. The explosion of non-state actors in the late 20th century broadened the scope of normative action on a global scale, from environmental activism to human rights advocacy, but at the same time, and by the same means, the same transnational processes broadened the scope for anti-cosmopolitan and for criminal activity.

The emergence of civil society organizations

NGOs (non-governmental organizations) and INGOs
(international non-governmental organizations) play a significant
role in filling service gaps in the provision of education, health and
welfare, disaster relief, and small-scale infrastructure development
left by governments with insufficient resources or insufficient
political will. But the roles of these organizations are much more
varied. Also referred to as CSOs (civil society organizations), they
pursue humanitarian missions and are distinct, in theory, from
purely political or economic associations or organizations.
Differentiated from protest movements, social clubs, and criminal
gangs by virtue of their non-economic and humanitarian social
objectives, these non-state actors have attracted significant
attention because of their capacity to influence and mobilize social
networks. Manuel Costoya's typology of CSOs distinguishes
between highly structured actors which warrant the title
'organization' and more amorphous 'movements'. Organized CSOs
have decision-making structures, delegated responsibilities,
budgets, and programmes. By contrast, social movements, such as
the World Social Forum, at which people gather for dialogue and
exchange of ideas about matters of common concern, are fluid,
inchoate, and volatile in the sense that they ebb and flow in tandem
with global issues and the shifting priorities of those who organize
them.

INGO categories

According to the UN Commission on Global Governance, a
non-governmental organization is classed as international when it
operates in three or more countries. Based upon this definition,
there were 28,900 identifiable international NGOs in 1993,
compared to a mere 176 in 1909. More recent analysis suggests a
much smaller number of 6,000 INGOs circa 2001, although this
reflects more exclusive criteria. There were an estimated 2,500
northern INGOs in 1990, indicating that the majority of INGOs,

with headquarters based in the developed word, are deployed in the 'Global South'; this includes affiliates of the major northern organizations like World Vision, CARE, Friends of the Earth, and more. Whatever the accurate number, these transnational actors have, in the areas of service delivery, won increased credence at the UN and the multilateral banks (the World Bank and regional development banks) which rely upon NGO/CSO assistance to implement development projects and gather 'local' information.

The end to the Cold War generated humanitarian crises in parts of the world previously inaccessible to Western governments and multilateral institutions, whereas I/NGOs could draw upon long-established social networks, were mobile, and, with avowedly neutral agencies like the International Red Cross and Médecins Sans Frontières, were able to operate in war zones. Added to this was an increase in development funds available to NGOs – from the World Bank especially – but also from public donations. Simply, transnational service and advocacy organizations complemented international development objectives at a time when the development agenda was lengthening.

Transnational corporations

Transnational corporations and corporations in general are viewed with suspicion in development circles. Transnational corporations (TNCs) are companies engaged in production across two or more international boundaries. Benefiting from the relatively open and stable international business environment in the West and Asia after 1945, TNCs grew rapidly in number and scale. By 2006, there were an estimated 78,000 such corporations, headquartered predominantly in Western Europe, North America, and Asia. Transnational companies routinely transfer materials, components, and completed products across national boundaries, and these 'internal' transfers account for a substantial proportion of world trade. Larger entities operate on an intercontinental scale, for example the Shell Corporation, which manages its up-stream and down-stream energy operations across more than 130 countries. It also met stiff opposition from NGOs such as Friends of the Earth Netherlands.

The Hague ruled in late 2009 that a Dutch court had, in fact, jurisdiction over the operations of Shell Nigeria. Friends of the Earth Netherlands, together with four farmers from Nigeria, filed the lawsuit against both Shell Nigeria and the Shell parent company in the Netherlands earlier in the year in order to expose the oil pollution in the Niger Delta, which had been targeted for crude oil extractions since the 1950s. The environmental damage to the region, caused by decades of indiscriminate petroleum waste dumping, was brought to the attention of the world by Nigerian author and environmental activist Ken Saro-Wiwa. Initially as a spokesman, and then as president, of the Movement for the Survivial of the Ogoni People, Saro-Wiwa led a non-violent campaign against environmental degradation of the land and waters of Ogoniland by the operation of the multinational petroleum industry, especially Shell. At the height of his non-violent campaign, he was arrested, tried by a special military tribunal, and was hanged in 1995 by the military government of General Sani Abacha, on charges widely viewed as political. His execution provoked international outrage and resulted in Nigeria's suspension from the Commonwealth of Nations for over three years. This is a classic, if ongoing, case study of a TNC being brought to heel by civil society intervention.

Meanwhile, motor vehicle manufacturers like Honda, Toyota, Ford, and General Motors manufacture and assemble motor vehicles in close proximity to major regional markets in Europe and Asia. Comparisons between national productivity and corporate sales revenues reveal that many of the world's major TNCs are as significant economic actors as many medium-sized countries. Their investments are eagerly sought after by national governments, for whom foreign direct investment equates to new employment and increased tax revenues. Corporations seek 'regulatory arbitrage' and exploit the weakened bargaining position of individual states competing with each other to attract lucrative investment dollars.

Foreign direct investment, from the West and from Japan and Korea, was a major factor in Asia's rapid late 20th-century economic growth, notably in Thailand and Vietnam. However, corporations stand accused by development, environmental, and human rights groups of engaging in practices detrimental to the wellbeing of people and communities across the developing world. To a limited extent, the *OECD Convention on the Bribery of Foreign Officials* drew attention within the global private sector to the damaging effects of corruption and the potential costs of bribery by companies headquartered in countries that are signatories to the convention. International efforts to bring to account companies that perpetrate or are complicit in environmental destruction, child labour exploitation, and political violence meet with stiff opposition from within the business community. Yet without cooperation from the transnational private sector, it is difficult to see how the UN millennium goals can be achieved.

During Annan's tenure as Secretary-General, the UN embarked upon a programme of business consultations under the umbrella of a 'Global Compact'. The considerable human and financial resources of transnational corporate actors and their undoubted influence could, it was thought, be harnessed towards the achievement of humanitarian objectives. Yet, the degree to which corporations, or private enterprise of any kind, can subscribe to such efforts is paradoxically limited by the nature of business competition. Free market advocates, like economist Milton Friedman, argue that the social responsibility of business is to be profitable, because from profits come employment, government revenues, and rising consumption. Yet, when the corrupt activities of corporations undermine United Nations programmes, such as the celebrated UN Iraq Oil-For-Food Program, or support brutal regimes in return for access to natural resources, not only do they contravene international law, they undermine human and global security.

Regional organizations

When the UN was founded, there were no significant regional institutions that could serve as a bridge between the global and the local. In terms of mediating global programmes for regional security, regional institutions are beginning to play a pivotal role in global governance. The region in which supranational institutional development is most advanced is Europe. Beginning with the European Coal and Steel Community, mutual gain through economic cooperation was the central dynamic in the formation, first, of the European Economic Community, then the European Community, and now the European Union (EU). Since the European Union's formation in 1993, membership has expanded from 12 to 25, with more countries applying to join. Enlargement, once derided by detractors, demonstrated the attraction of economic security in numbers – especially for the smaller European states.

The European Council of Ministers, European Commission, and Parliament have acquired some of the sovereign functions of member states. The EU can enact binding laws with regard to welfare provision, human rights, minimum wages, environmental standards, food safety standards, and more. After failing at its formation in 1993 to deal effectively with the break-up of the former Yugoslavia, the EU has matured as a regional security actor. The EU is moving towards a 'security community' in Europe in which the Union, rather than member states acting as sovereign entities, pursues a European foreign policy and increasingly a security role in Europe and Africa. In 2003, a EU peacekeeping force was stationed in FYR Macedonia to stabilize the country after a brief civil war in 2001. Signalling a determination to play a more active regional security role, the EU now maintains a multinational standing 'ready-response' force of 1,500 soldiers to deal with strategic

13. Civil society diplomacy: Amnesty International Secretary-General Irene Khan (left) and EU Foreign Policy Chief Javier Solana (right), 15 April 2008

and humanitarian crises – in Europe, but also in northern and sub-Saharan Africa.

Regional organizations are becoming increasingly active, perhaps in recognition that an under-resourced UN system needs assistance to implement its security mandate at the regional and national levels. The EU and the less well known but influential OSCE (Organization for Security and Cooperation in Europe) is the most extensive European security organization in that it includes Russia as the successor to the Soviet Union. With the North Atlantic Treaty Organization (NATO) incorporating the USA, the OSCE's mission is evolving from being a facilitator of security dialogue and a promoter of democratization to engagement in the business of peacekeeping. According to Nina Graeger and Alexandra Novosseloff, this organization 'is the most important norm-building organization in Europe', although this

14. Civil unrest in Africa: men belonging to the Kisii tribe run in a field as they battle a group of Kalenjin tribespeople in the western Kenyan town of Chebilat, 3 February 2008

effectiveness is limited by renewed strategic rivalry between the USA and Russia.

In sum, globalization increases the potency of transnational linkages and exposes national societies to a greater array of international shocks and security risks. Internally, many new states face the twin demands of developing viable political institutions while competing for survival in a 'hyperglobalizing' global economy. This is the diplomatic challenge, not only for the Global South, but also for the developed world. It has also made modern diplomacy at once more challenging and complex. It is a brave new world.

References and further reading

Preface

David Reynolds's observation on the origins of diplomacy is in *Summits: Six Meetings That Shaped the Twentieth Century* (Basic Books, 2007). The Toynbee and Kissinger quotes are found in Daniel M. Smith and Joseph M. Siracusa, *The Testing of America, 1914–1945* (Forum Press, 1979) and Henry Kissinger, *Diplomacy* (Simon and Schuster, 1994), respectively.

Chapter 1

To begin at the beginning, see Harold Nicolson's faded – and fading – classic, *Diplomacy* (Harcourt Brace, 1939), which is not to be confused with Henry Kissinger's otherwise brilliant diplomatic history, *Diplomacy* (Simon and Schuster, 1994), which, Kissinger assures us, is quite different in scope, intentions, and ideas. Indispensable is M. S. Anderson's treatise on the evolution of diplomacy to 1919, *The Rise of Modern Diplomacy, 1450–1919* (Longman, 1993). The history of diplomacy is admirably covered in G. R. Berridge, *Diplomacy: Theory and Practice*, 4th edn. (Palgrave Macmillan, 2009); Keith Hamilton and Richard Langhorne, *The Practice of Diplomacy: Its Evolution, Theory and Administration*, 2nd edn. (Routledge, 2010); and Adam Watson, *Diplomacy: Dialogue between States* (Routledge, 1982). For a critique of the culture of traditional diplomatic services, see Shaun Riordan, *The New Diplomacy* (Polity Press, 2002).

How diplomats represent state institutions in a complex relationship of facts designed to bring order to international society is explored in *The Diplomatic Corps as an Institution of International Society*, ed. Paul Sharp and Geoffrey Wiseman (Palgrave Macmillan, 2008). G. R. Berridge has much to say in *Return to the United Nations: UN Diplomacy in Regional Conflicts* (Palgrave Macmillan, 1991). For the emerging diplomacy of civil society, see Paul Battersby and Joseph M. Siracusa, *Globalization and Human Security* (Rowman and Littlefield, 2009). Quotes on public diplomacy are taken from Charles Wolf, Jr, and Brian Rosen, *Public Diplomacy: How To Think About It and Improve It* (RAND, 2004). Also useful is Walter R. Roberts, 'The Evolution of Diplomacy', *Mediterranean Quarterly*, 17 (Summer 2006): 55.

For the history and significance of treaties, see Charles L. Philips and Alan Axelrod (eds.), *Encyclopedia of Historical Treaties and Alliances*, 2 vols (Facts on File, 2001); J. A. S. Grenville, *The Major International Treaties, 1914–1973: A History and Guide with Texts* (Methuen, 1974); Mario Toscano, *The History of Treaties and International Politics* (Johns Hopkins University Press, 1966); and Eileen Denza, *Diplomatic Law*, 3rd edn. (Oxford University Press, 2008).

Chapter 2

The best summary of the diplomacy of the American Revolution is Samuel Flagg Bemis, *The Diplomacy of the American Revolution* (D. Appleton-Century, 1935). Bemis skilfully exploits archives in offering a Whig interpretation of an innocent America dealing with corrupt Europe. This interpretation has been challenged, but not the coverage and detailed analysis. Also useful are Jonathan R. Dull, *A Diplomatic History of the American Revolution* (Yale University Press, 1985); Reginald Horsman, *The Diplomacy of the New Republic* (Harlan Davidson, 1985); and Robert R. Palmer, *The Age of the Democratic Revolution: A Political History of Europe and America, 1760–1800*, Vol. 1: *The Challenge* (Princeton University Press, 1959).

Arthur M. Schlesinger's *The Colonial Merchants and the American Revolution, 1763–1776* (Longmans, 1918) is a landmark study of the origins of the American Revolution, showing the role merchants played in staving off radical measures of Parliament and colonials until 1776.

The best general account of British ministerial politics and the American question for 1773 to 1775 is Bernard Donoughue, *British Politics and the American Revolution, the Path to War, 1773–75* (Macmillan, 1964). For a description of British military objectives and successes, see Piers Mackesy, *The War for America, 1775–1783* (University of Nebraska Press, 1993). William C. Stinchcombe, *The American Revolution and the French Alliance* (Syracuse University Press, 1969) analyses the domestic reaction to the French alliance in America, making the case that colonial Americans suspended their traditional anti-French and anti-Catholic beliefs to make it a success. For a discussion of domestic and international factors and influences, consult Richard W. Van Alstyne, *Empire and Independence: The International History of the American Revolution* (John Wiley, 1965).

Benjamin Franklin was the most important diplomat of the American Revolution and because of this has attracted much scholarly attention. The best studies of Franklin and his times are Claude A. Lopez and Eugenia W. Herbert, *The Private Franklin: The Man and His Family* (Norton, 1975); Gerald Stourzh, *Benjamin Franklin and American Foreign Policy* (University of Chicago Press, 1954); and Carl Van Doren, *Benjamin Franklin* (Viking, 1938).

The standard account of Henry Laurens, John Adams, Benjamin Franklin, and particularly John Jay, who negotiated the peace with Great Britain in 1782, is Richard B. Morris, *The Peacemakers: The Great Powers and American Independence* (Harper and Row, 1965). This well-researched work is marred only by the author's excessive distrust of Vergennes and Europeans in general. Valuable insights are found in Lawrence S. Kaplan, 'The Treaty of Paris 1783: A Historiographical Challenge', *International History Review*, 5 (August 1983): 431–42; and Ronald Hoffman and Peter J. Albert (eds.), *Peace and Peacemakers: The Treaty of 1783* (University of Virginia Press for the United States Capitol Historical Society, 1986). The Royal Instructions to the Peace Commission of 1778 are conveniently located in S. E. Morison (ed.), *Sources and Documents Illustrating the American Revolution, 1764–1788* (The Clarendon Press, 1923).

Chapter 3

The best general introductions to European history covered by this chapter are Norman Rich, *Great Power Diplomacy, 1814–1914*

(McGraw-Hill, 1992); A. J. P. Taylor, *The Struggle for Mastery in Europe, 1848–1918* (Oxford University Press, 1954); Christopher J. Bartlett, *The Global Conflict: The International Rivalry of the Great Powers, 1880–1990* (Longman, 1994); Norman Stone, *Europe Transformed, 1878–1919* (Oxford University Press, 1999); and James Joll, *Europe since 1870*, 4th edn. (Penguin, 1990). Nineteenth-century diplomacy is treated in Christopher J. Bartlett, *Peace, War and the European Powers, 1814–1914* (Palgrave Macmillan, 1996); and F. R. Bridge and Roger Bullen, *The Great Powers and the European States System, 1815–1914* (Longman, 1980). Useful access to primary source material is provided by Ralph R. Menning (ed.), *The Art of the Possible: Documents on Great Power Diplomacy, 1814–1914* (McGraw-Hill, 1996).

For the breakdown of Bismarck's alliance system, see Richard Langhorne, *The Collapse of the Concert of Europe: International Politics, 1890–1914* (Palgrave Macmillan, 1981); William L. Langer, *The Franco-Russian Alliance, 1890–1894* (Harvard University Press, 1929) and *The Diplomacy of Imperialism*, 2nd edn. (Knopf, 1968); and George F. Kennan, *The Decline of Bismarck's European Order: Franco-Russian Relations, 1875–1890* (Princeton University Press, 1979). James Joll and Gordon Martel's *The Origins of the First World War*, 3rd edn. (Oxford University Press, 2006) remains the best general introduction to the subject, while the best military history of World War I is B. H. Liddell Hart, *History of the First World War* (Weidenfeld and Nicolson, 1970). For the harm done on the ground level, see Alan Kramer, *Dynamic of Destruction: Culture and Mass Killing in the First World War* (Oxford University Press, 2007); and Alexander Watson, *Enduring the Great War: Combat, Morale and Collapse in the German and British Armies, 1914–1918* (Cambridge University Press, 2008).

For the entry of the United States into the war and its subsequent rejection of the Treaty of Versailles, see Thomas J. Knock, *To End All Wars: Woodrow Wilson and the Quest for a New World Order* (Princeton University Press, 1995); Daniel M. Smith, *The Great Departure: United States and World War I, 1914–1920* (Wiley, 1965); and Arthur S. Link, *Wilson, the Diplomatist* (Johns Hopkins University Press, 1957).

For Germany's 'September Program', see Fritz Fischer, *Germany's War Aims in the First World War* (Norton, 1967). Fischer lays the blame for war squarely on Berlin. John A. Moses's *The Politics of Illusion: The Fischer Controversy in German Historiography* (Barnes and Noble, 1975) presents a detailed review of Fischer's revisionist thesis. Jay Winter and Antoine Prost's *The Great War in History: Debates and Controversies, 1914 to the Present* (Cambridge University Press, 2006) is an important comparative study, analysing a multitude of books on World War I written by French, British, and German scholars in order to show patterns of themes and methods over time.

For the historical debate surrounding the course and consequences of the Treaty of Versailles, see Manfred F. Boemeke, Gerald D. Feldman, and Elisabeth Glaser (eds.), *The Treaty of Versailles: A Reassessment after 75 Years* (Cambridge University Press, 1998). Quotes by David Lloyd George, Winston Churchill, and John Maynard Keynes in this chapter are found in David Lloyd George, *British War Aims* (George H. Doran, 1917) and *War Memoirs* (Little Brown, 1932–7); Winston Churchill, *The World Crisis* (Butterworth, 1923–31), vol. 5; and John Maynard Keynes, *The Economic Consequences of the Peace* (Harcourt, Brace and Howe, 1920), respectively.

Chapter 4

Before all else, I should like to pay tribute to John Lukacs, whose 'The Night Stalin and Churchill Divided Europe', *The New York Times Magazine*, 5 October 1969, 37–50, inspired a generation of scholarship, including my own. See Joseph M. Siracusa, *Into the Dark House: American Diplomacy and the Ideological Origins of the Cold War* (Regina Books, 1998) and 'The Meaning of TOLSTOY: Churchill, Stalin, and the Balkans, Moscow, October 1944', *Diplomatic History*, 3 (Fall 1979), 443–63, which is a discussion of the source material for this meeting located in the Public Record Office. Also useful are Albert Resis, 'The Churchill-Stalin Secret "Percentages" Agreement on the Balkans, Moscow, October 1944', *American Historical Review*, 85 (1981), 368–87, and 'Spheres of Influence in Soviet Diplomacy', *Journal of Modern History*, 53 (1981), 417–39; and Vojtech Mastny, *Russia's Road to the Cold War: Diplomacy, Warfare, and the Politics of Communism, 1941–1945* (Columbia University Press, 1979).

Recommended overviews of the war years include the first volume in Norman A. Graebner, Richard Dean Burns, and Joseph M. Siracusa, *America and the Cold War, 1941–1991: A Realist Interpretation*, 2 vols (Praeger Security International, 2010); Gerhard L. Weinberg, *A World at Arms: A Global History of World War II* (Cambridge University Press, 1994); William H. McNeill, *America, Britain and Russia: Their Cooperation and Conflict, 1941–1946* (Oxford University Press, 1953); Herbert Feis, *Churchill, Roosevelt, Stalin: The War They Waged and the Peace They Sought* (Princeton University Press, 1957); and John L. Snell, *Illusion and Necessity: The Diplomacy of Global War, 1939–1945* (Houghton Mifflin, 1963). On the British side, see Sir Lleywellyn Woodard, *History of the Second World War: British Foreign Policy in the Second World* War, 5 vols (HMSO, 1970–6) and John Charmley, *Churchill's Grand Alliance: The Anglo-American Special Relationship, 1940–57* (Hodder and Stoughton, 1995). The best reference work for the period is *The Oxford Companion to the Second World War*, ed. I. C. B. Dear (Oxford University Press, 1995).

Winston Churchill's recollection of events is found in Chapter 15, 'October in Moscow', in *The Second World War*, vol. 6, *Triumph and Tragedy* (Houghton Mifflin, 1953). Also useful are *The Diaries of Sir Alexander Cadogan, 1939–45*, ed. David Dilks (Cassell, 1971); Anthony Eden, *The Memoirs of Anthony Eden, Earl of Avon: The Reckoning* (Houghton Mifflin, 1965); W. Averell Harriman and Elie Abel, *Special Envoy to Churchill and Stalin, 1941–1946* (Random House, 1975); R. E. Sherwood, *Roosevelt and Hopkins: An Intimate History* (Putnam's, 1977); Charles E. Bohlen, *Witness to History, 1929–1969* (Norton, 1973); and George F. Kennan, *Memoirs, 1925–1963* (Little, Brown, 1967).

Chapter 5

That Australian scholars have been talking and writing about the United States far more than American scholars have been talking and writing about Australia should come as no surprise. See Joseph M. Siracusa, 'The United Sates, Australia, and the Central Pacific', in *Guide to American Foreign Relations since 1700*, ed. Richard Dean Burns (ABC-CLIO, 1983). Also see Joseph M. Siracusa and Yeong-Han Cheong, *America's Australia/Australia's America: A Guide to Issues and References* (Regina Books, 1997); and Joseph M. Siracusa and David G. Coleman, *Australia Looks to*

America: Australian–American Relations since Pearl Harbor (Regina Books, 2006).

For general background, see C. Hartley Grattan, *The United States and the Southwest Pacific* (Harvard University Press, 1961); Warner Levi, *American–Australian Relations* (University of Minnesota Press, 1947); and Gordon Greenwood, *Early Australian–American Relations* (Melbourne University Press, 1944).

Trevor R. Reese's *Australia, New Zealand, and the United States* (Oxford University Press, 1969) provides a broad survey of the conclusion and operation of the ANZUS Treaty, while Joseph G. Starke's *ANZUS Treaty Alliance* (Melbourne University Press, 1965) remains the classic treatment of the subject.

Also useful are Harry C. Gelber, *The Australian–American Alliance: Costs and Benefits* (Penguin, 1968); Henry S. Albinski, *ANZUS, the United States and Pacific Security* (University Press of America, 1987); and Coral Bell, *Dependent Ally: A Study in Australian Foreign Policy* (Oxford University Press, 1988).

Memoir literature includes D. Dilks (ed.), *The Diaries of Sir Alexander Cadogan, 1938–45* (Cassell, 1971); Walter Millis (ed.), *The Forrestal Diaries: The Inner History of the Cold War* (Cassell, 1952); and P. C. Spender, *Exercises in Diplomacy: The ANZUS Treaty and the Colombo Plan* (Sydney University Press, 1969). Primary documents for ANZUS may be found in *The ANZUS Documents*, ed. A. Burnett (Australian National University, 1991) and *Australian–American Relations since 1945*, ed. Glen St J. Barclay and Joseph M. Siracusa (Holt, Rinehart and Winston, 1976).

Chapter 6

Portions of this chapter have been adapted from my recent study, with Paul Battersby, *Globalization and Human Security* (Rowman and Littlefield, 2009).

The concept of globalization has gathered a rich bibliography in a relatively short period of time and become embedded in the social science lexicon. A good general and brief study of globalization is Manfred Steger's *Globalization: A Very Short Introduction* (Oxford

University Press, 2003). For a comprehensive and multi-layered introduction, see John Baylis and Steve Smith (eds.), *The Globalization of World Politics: An Introduction to International Relations* (Oxford University Press, 2001). Baylis and Smith bring together authored chapters on history, political theory, conflict and security, international institutions, environmental politics, and human rights.

For the economic dimensions of globalization, see Jurgen Osterhammel, Niels Petersen, and Donna Geyer, *Globalization: A Short History* (Princeton University Press, 2005); Niall Ferguson, *The Cash Nexus: Money and Power in the Modern World* (Basic Books, 2001); and Erich Rauchway, *Blessed among Nations: How the World Made America* (Hill and Wang, 2006).

The processes of what we recognize as globalization span several centuries. For different historical perspectives, see David Held, Anthony McGrew, David Goldblatt, and Jonathan Perraton, *Global Transformations: Politics, Economics, and Culture* (Stanford University Press, 1999). Also useful are Anthony Giddens, *The Consequences of Modernity* (Polity Press, 1990) and *Runaway World* (Routledge, 2000); Frederic Jameson and Massao Mioyshi (eds.), *The Cultures of Globalization* (Duke University Press, 1998); and James H. Mittleman (ed.), *The Globalization Syndrome* (Princeton University Press, 2000).

For critical perspectives on human security, see Giorgio Shani, Makoto Sato, and Mustapha Kamal Pasha (eds.), *Protecting Human Security in a Post 9/11 World: Critical and Global Insights* (Palgrave Macmillan, 2007). Also see International Commission on Intervention and State Sovereignty, *The Responsibility to Protect* (International Development Research Center, 2001); and Andrew Mack, *The Human Security Report 2005: War and Peace in the 21st Century* (Oxford University Press, 2005).

The quotes in this chapter may be found in Nicholas Stern, *The Stern Review: The Economics of Climate Change* (HM Treasury, 2006); Roland Paris, 'Human Security: Paradigm Shift or Hot Air?', in *New Global Dangers: Changing Dimensions of International Security*, ed. M. E. Brown, O. R. Cote, Jr, S. M. Lynn-Jones, and S. E. Miller (MIT Press, 2004); Jim Whitman, *The Limits of Global Governance* (Routledge, 2005); Manuel Mejido Costoya, *Toward a Typology of*

Civil Actors: The Case of the Movement to Change International Trade Rules and Barriers (United Nations Research Institute for Social Development, 2007); and Nina Graeger and Alexandra Novosseloff, 'The Role of the OSCE and the EU', in *The United Nations and Regional Security: Europe and Beyond*, ed. Michael Pugh and Waheguru Pal Singh Sidhu (Lynne Rienner, 2003).

Index

CLASSICS
A Very Short Introduction
Mary Beard and John Henderson

This Very Short Introduction to Classics links a haunting temple on a lonely mountainside to the glory of ancient Greece and the grandeur of Rome, and to Classics within modern culture – from Jefferson and Byron to Asterix and Ben-Hur.

'The authors show us that Classics is a "modern" and sexy subject. They succeed brilliantly in this regard ... nobody could fail to be informed and entertained – and the accent of the book is provocative and stimulating.'

John Godwin, *Times Literary Supplement*

'Statues and slavery, temples and tragedies, museum, marbles, and mythology – this provocative guide to the Classics demystifies its varied subject-matter while seducing the reader with the obvious enthusiasm and pleasure which mark its writing.'

Edith Hall

ARCHAEOLOGY
A Very Short Introduction
Paul Bahn

This entertaining Very Short Introduction reflects the enduring popularity of archaeology – a subject which appeals as a pastime, career, and academic discipline, encompasses the whole globe, and surveys 2.5 million years. From deserts to jungles, from deep caves to mountain tops, from pebble tools to satellite photographs, from excavation to abstract theory, archaeology interacts with nearly every other discipline in its attempts to reconstruct the past.

'very lively indeed and remarkably perceptive ... a quite brilliant and level-headed look at the curious world of archaeology'

Barry Cunliffe, University of Oxford

'It is often said that well-written books are rare in archaeology, but this is a model of good writing for a general audience. The book is full of jokes, but its serious message – that archaeology can be a rich and fascinating subject – it gets across with more panache than any other book I know.'

Simon Denison, editor of *British Archaeology*

www.oup.co.uk/vsi/archaeology

MUSIC
A Very Short Introduction
Nicholas Cook

This stimulating Very Short Introduction to music invites us to really *think* about music and the values and qualities we ascribe to it.

> 'A *tour de force*. Nicholas Cook is without doubt one of the most probing and creative thinkers about music we have today.'
>
> **Jim Samson, University of Bristol**

> 'Nicholas Cook offers a perspective that is clearly influenced by recent writing in a host of disciplines related to music. It may well prove a landmark in the appreciation of the topic ... In short, I can hardly imagine it being done better.'
>
> **Roger Parker, University of Cambridge**

www.oup.co.uk/vsi/music